Curious Christians

Curious Christians

David H. C. Read

ABINGDON PRESS
Nashville
and
New York

CURIOUS CHRISTIANS

Library of Congress Cataloging in Publication Data

READ, DAVID HAXTON CARSWELL. Curious Christians. 1. Pres-
byterian church—Sermons. 2. Sermons, American. I. Title.
BX9178.R367C87   1973   252′.05′242   72-5201

ISBN 0-687-10101-8

Scripture quotations noted RSV are from the Revised Standard
Version of the Bible, copyrighted 1946 and 1952 by the
Division of Christian Education, National Council of Churches,
and are used by permission.

MANUFACTURED BY THE PARTHENON PRESS AT
NASHVILLE, TENNESSEE, UNITED STATES OF AMERICA

*For my Mother
in her hundredth year*

Preface

Curiosity may have killed the cat, but it is what keeps most of us alive. If there is anything more entrancing than the curiosity of an infant, it is the continuing curiosity of one who is very old.

Not too much has been written about this instinct as a gateway to vital religion in spite of the examples in the Bible and the insistence of Jesus on the childlike spirit of wonder and inquiry. These talks were born out of my "curiosity about curiosity," and I hope some may find them a stimulus to fresh discovery. They are addressed to all who are in any way open to the adventure of faith. Only the musclebound atheist or the bigoted believer is impervious to any invitation to explore the unseen world.

I write from specific Christian convictions. But I want to say with Paul: "I press on, hoping to take hold of that for which Christ once took hold of me. . . . I do not reckon myself to have got hold of it yet."

I am grateful to the company of the curious in my own church and in the National Radio Pulpit family who stimulate my mind and spirit, and to my secretary, Carolyn Mathis, who in addition efficiently oversees the transfer of these thoughts to print.

These addresses were first presented on the National Radio Pulpit program, produced by NBC Radio in association with the Broadcasting and Film Commission of the National Council of Churches, whom I thank for permission to print in this form.

David H. C. Read

Contents

CONTENTS

1

Religion in the Seventies – The New Curiosity

The only safe remark to make about the state of religion in America in the seventies is that it is one of tremendous confusion. In the forties and early fifties we could talk about a remarkable expansion of religious affiliation with new churches springing up all over the country, church rolls swelling, great popular support for religious causes, and books of popular piety hitting the best-seller lists. By the time of the sixties this boom not only had leveled off, but there was a noticeable decline in enthusiasm for organized religion, in church attendance and in general acceptance of conventional belief. In the public estimation religion slumped dramatically as an important factor in society, and those who still gave it high priority were shocked to find that church leaders themselves seemed to have lost confidence and were voicing aloud their inmost doubts about not only the structure but the basic beliefs of the Church. This was the period that culminated in the now forgotten theology of the "death of God."

You might expect that the seventies would simply continue this trend, with religion falling farther and farther into the background and a spirit of secularism taking over. After all, our radical theologians were always talking about the impossibility of talking to modern man about God and the supernatural, and it would seem natural to expect that in another decade only the old and conventional would retain any semblance of traditional religious belief. But in fact, something very different seems to be happening.

It is true, as I have said, that confusion reigns on the religious scene today; but it is simply not true that religion itself is on the way out. On the contrary, there is a remarkable outburst of what I am going to call religious curiosity, and an intense new interest in the very things that the experts had said were of little interest to the modern mind. While organized religion in the form of conventional church activities is still under a cloud, religion itself—the question of God, of the supernatural, of spiritual and mystical experience, of the person of Jesus Christ, of prayer, even of miracle—has come alive with astonishing force and intensity. The generation that was supposed to find religious symbols and spiritual values meaningless and absurd is revolting from the materialism of a secular society and wallowing in every kind of religious activity from the most exalted and ennobling to the most crudely superstitious. College students may stay away from chapel in droves, but they are demanding courses in religion as never before. On the bookracks, jostling among the cookbooks and the pornography, you will find Kierkegaard, Tillich, Kahlil Gibran, St. Augustine, and the Koran—not to mention the immense output of the revived religion of astrology. When the Bible Society's paperback *Today's English Version of the New Testament* reaches a world record of over 25 million copies sold, someone must be reading it, and almost every month some new Bible translation hits the headlines. At one end of the theological spectrum you find a passionate devotion to such exotic cults as "Krishna Consciousness," while at the other, a new form of Christian revivalism sweeps hundreds of thousands into the "Jesus movement."

Religious topics creep into ordinary conversation far more than they did a few years ago, and curiosity about God and questions of belief break out in the most unexpected places. The world of music and the theater is invaded by such productions as *Jesus Christ Superstar,* and *Godspell,* while novels are appearing that break with the tired cynicism and sterile secularism of recent years

13

and are crammed with religious symbolism and spiritual curiosity.

This, then, is the unexpected mood of the seventies. I say "unexpected," for the intellectual climate of fifty years ago hardly seemed to indicate that religion would be a live concern as this century draws to its close. The projections of writers like H. G. Wells and Bertrand Russell didn't leave much room for religion as they saw mankind moving either to its apotheosis or its doom.

There used to be a theory, you know, that religion flourishes in a climate of ignorance and naïveté and, therefore, will inevitably decline and disappear as human beings become smarter and more sophisticated. Belief in God was supposed to be a primitive way of explaining the mysteries of the universe before science came along to show us how everything really works. Trust in a heavenly Father was said to be a hangover from the infancy of mankind, doomed to disappear as men and women became more mature and independent. According to this theory, it is only a matter of time before religion with its apparatus of worship, prayers, priests, and ceremonies will vanish as completely as the dinosaur from the face of the earth. Its exit is only delayed by such factors as the nostalgia of the old and the cynical exploitation of the religious instincts by those who find it useful to keep the poor and the oppressed satisfied with misery on earth in the hope of a better time in heaven.

This theory, which was based on a superficial reading of the seamier side of church history, never did make much sense. For not only have most of the intellectual giants of human enlightenment— from Erasmus through Pascal, Kant, and Kierkegaard to Buber, Tillich, and Niebuhr—been religious believers, but the development of modern science itself was fostered by the Judeo-Christian outlook on life. Today the theory can only be held as a dogma. It still, as we know, forms part of Marxist orthodoxy, but the reports we are receiving from communist countries and much of the underground literature being produced there show that the new generation is by no means satisfied with this crude elimination of the religious dimension from human life.

What is happening today finally disposes of the notion that mere technological progress will inevitably eliminate religion from the human scene. It is just when we have been conditioned to expect almost anything from the scientist and technician, just when we have seen such fantastic achievements as the exploration of space and journeys to the moon, just when man seems to have gained an unprecedented control of the sources of power, just when an immense expansion of human brain-power seems on the horizon that we are witnessing a unique revival of religion. A whole generation seems to be stepping away from the bright dreams of scientific humanism and seeking light from the prophets and mystics, and from all kinds of religion, new and old. What this indicates is not, as some might want to say, a temporary case of "future shock"—a scare-reaction from the dangers that accompany the acceleration of man's control over nature—but surely a fresh realization that no amount of human progress in the field of "know-how" can eliminate the eternal question of the "know-why." In other words we are experiencing a rebirth of the fundamental religious questions concerning the meaning of life. "Who am I?" "Where did we come from?" "Where are we going?" And, "Why should I choose one way rather than another?" It is because religion offers some kind of answer to these questions that the present generation has become inquisitive as to what these answers may be.

This is what I call the "new curiosity." It is the mark of our age. It is as if we had passed through the period when religion was regarded either as a fading force doomed to disappear, or else as a familiar landmark to which one paid occasional respect. More and more people are becoming aware that religion lies right at the center of the current concern for new values by which to live and new insights into the meaning of human life. And there is a growing realization that religion offers that extra dimension, that heightened consciousness, that inward enlightenment for which the spirit of man is groping today. If this movement often seems to be bypassing the conventional churches, our job as churchmen is not to deplore and to criticize but to ask ourselves whether in fact, in our worship, our presentation of the gospel, and our social activities, we have not obscured the excitement of the religious quest and muffled the note of divine transcendence. It looks as though much of our effort has gone into a secularizing of the Christian gospel, a constant explaining away of the mysteries of the faith, and an attempt to commend religion as socially desirable and psychologically useful. When youth reject the churches, it is not always because of an urge to abandon moral restraints and go their own way. Sometimes it is because they find more spiritual satisfaction, more experience of the transcendent, beyond the confines of organized religion.

The new curiosity indicates a new look at the whole question of religious belief and practice. It is, therefore, not necessarily a bad thing that there is some confusion in the churches at the present time. For we are awakening to the fact that we have not been nearly curious enough about the doctrines we have been taught or the religious habits in which we have been trained. We are realizing that Christianity is not a neatly packaged religion about which nothing more is to be said, and that there is an enormous field for exploration

17

in our ways of worship, our devotional life, and our practical interpretation of the gospel. What is needed now is for the spirit of curiosity to break loose within the framework of the organized churches, so that the religious inquirer may find a welcome and not feel that he is among those whose minds are frozen and for whom religion has no real mystery left.

I want to speak in this book about how this spirit of curiosity can work among the accepted doctrines and practices of the Christian church. But at this point it would be well to raise the question as to whether religious curiosity is always as healthful and hopeful as I seem to be suggesting.

I think we have to make a distinction here. Certainly, active religious curiosity is infinitely preferable to an attitude of either thoughtless acceptance or equally thoughtless rejection. But there is a distinction to be made between this lively desire to discover spiritual truth and experience the grace of God, and the attitude of mind we know as idle curiosity. There is a kind of dilettante approach to religion that is the very opposite of the active curiosity I have been talking about.

There is, for instance, the kind of person who takes up religion as a kind of hobby—often an alternative to golf or bridge as an interest for days of leisure and retirement. Such a person is liable to be caught up in speculations about the end of the world and readily falls victim to any new movement that offers startling revelations about who is going to be saved and when the end will come. I call their absorption with such subjects idle curiosity because it produces no fruit of the spirit in their lives and leads to no practical demonstration of Christian love. We are all given at times to a barren curiosity about matters beyond our powers of comprehension. There is nothing idle about the cry of the bereaved for a word about life after death, but there are plenty of idle questions that people ask about conditions beyond the grave. I note that Jesus took with the utmost seriousness the cry of a young man: "Master, what shall I do to inherit eternal life?" but that he refused to answer the trick question that was put to him about a woman whose seven husbands had predeceased her: "At the resurrection whose wife is she to be?" The Bible respects the question: "If a man die shall he live again?" but discourages idle curiosity about conditions in a dimension we cannot possibly understand. The sound rule is given in the book of Ecclesiasticus: "Be not curious in unnecessary matters."

There is also an idle curiosity that is the speciality of the academic. I am talking now about those for whom speculation is a way of life—or rather, a way of *observing* life. The book of Acts, commenting on Paul's visit to Athens, remarks that "all the Athenians and strangers which were there

19

spend their time in nothing else, but either to tell, or to hear some new thing" (Acts 17:21). It is possible that some current religious curiosity has no more serious basis than this. It can be as amusing to investigate men's ideas of God as it is to discuss the possibility of life on other planets—and as unprofitable. The discovery that theology can be fun too is not quite the same thing as entering the kingdom of God.

Religious curiosity is idle when it leads to no life-changing decision. Just as a girl knows the difference between the young man whose curiosity about her has serious intent and the philanderer who is just "playing the field," so we may presume that God can distinguish between idle and active religious curiosity. The religious philanderer has no intention of being hooked. This kind of curiosity is often a device for avoiding the challenge of living religion. At the moment there is an intense interest in the person of Jesus Christ. Insofar as this leads a man or woman to real confrontation with him and to the challenge to become a disciple, this curiosity is active and inspired. But it can be deflected into a mere intellectual exercise, an indulgence in a popular fad.

Jesus himself, in commending an attitude of active curiosity, emphasized that it would lead to decision and discovery: "Seek, and you will find." He is not offering some religious game for the unemployed. He is promising that the sincere and wholehearted seeker after God and his kingdom will find a response. Curiosity then must have this determination behind it, this readiness to accept what is revealed. "Blessed are the pure in heart, for they shall see God."

If this spirit lies behind the new curiosity of the seventies, we may yet see a revival of religion of totally unexpected depth and power.

2

Curious Christians

Sometime in the thirties there was a play running in London which contained a line that has never been forgotten. When one of the characters said: "That's funny," the reply was: "Do you mean funny-peculiar or funny ha-ha?" Well, it occurs to me that when you hear the title "Curious Christians," you may want to ask: "Do you mean curious-peculiar or curious-inquiring?" So let me hasten to say that the theme of this chapter is Christian curiosity and not Christian eccentrics and oddballs. There are such around, of course, and most of us could discourse on some very peculiar Christians we have met. But what I want to speak about is curiosity, or the spirit of lively inquiry, as a key to religious health.

If it's true that we are living in a period of fresh and lively interest in religion, especially among the younger generation, we should expect this curiosity to be reflected within the churches. But, on the whole, it isn't—and this may be one reason why so many today who are newly aware of the divine dimension and hungry for some real spiritual experience are bypassing the churches. Among the thousands who stroll past church doors on Sunday morning without ever a thought of going in, there must be many with genuine religious aspirations and belief in God. They are not all atheists, agnostics, and secularists. Why, then, does it not occur to them that within the church building there might be some possibility of a new encounter with God, of satisfying this hunger of the soul? One of the reasons, I believe, is that they picture the organized churches as petrified institutions. A Christian congregation, they think, consists of people whose minds were made up years ago, who repeat well-worn creeds and prayers, sing familiar hymns, and haven't had a new religious thought since they were confirmed. They're not curious any more: they've got it all wrapped up.

Now this is a caricature of the congregations I happen to know. There's far more diversity of belief, more wondering, far more inquiry going on in the average church than even the pastor knows—let alone the outside observer. But there is sufficient truth in the accusation to make us who are church men and women sit up and take notice. Nothing would transform the life of our

23

religious institutions more quickly than an outburst of real, live curiosity. We suffer from the spirit of mild acceptance, of "don't disturb me," of letting sleeping dogmas lie. It is on the fringe of the church, among those who are what we call "nominal members," that this lack of curiosity is most obvious, but even regular worshipers succumb to this paralysis of the inquiring mind. So we give the impression that to be a member of a church means the end of the religious quest. How much more exciting it appears to remain outside and continue to ask, to seek, and to knock.

That was a quotation from Jesus, you know. This is the command and the promise he gave to his disciples: "Ask, and you will receive, seek and you will find; knock, and the door will be opened." These words are valid for all of us and for all time. This is what he is telling us about the nature of faith and Christian commitment. Instead of marking the end of the religious quest it should mean a constant new beginning. If only we could discover what it means in this sense to be a "curious Christian," and if only we could communicate the excitement of this discovery to the modern world, then there would be tremendous days ahead for the church.

The curious Christian is one who is always alert for new discovery and understanding. He doesn't imagine that he now knows all he ever will about God. He expects to find out more about

Jesus Christ every year. For him the Holy Spirit is not a blurred and lifeless phrase but a reality he wants to experience. He is inquisitive about the nature of true prayer, conscious that he has only paddled on the edges of this vast ocean of spiritual potential. He realizes that the Bible is an inexhaustible book and is curious about the new ways in which he keeps hearing in it the word of God. He wonders how worship can become more active and lively for modern Christians. And he is endlessly inquisitive about what the church calls "the means of grace."

Later I hope to talk about some of these specific areas of curiosity. Now, I am concentrating on the spirit of inquiry, on the overarching command to keep asking, to keep seeking, to keep knocking at the door.

When Jesus commended the childlike spirit, saying: "Unless you turn and become like children, you will never enter the kingdom of heaven" (Matthew 18:3 RSV), no doubt those who heard him thought like us that he was referring to the attitude of trust, of dependence, of receptivity, and of simplicity. And so, I am sure, he was. But I am beginning to realize that he must also have had in mind another characteristic of childhood—namely curiosity. From the moment of birth a child is endlessly curious. We have in our home a three-year-old who is inquisitive about everything from a shower of rain to the contents of my desk. He takes nothing for granted, and so life is a series of delightful surprises from morning to night. I find myself catching the infection of curiosity and beginning to wonder again about a host of things that grown-up people just accept as part of the landscape. Jesus indicated that we need to recapture this mood whatever age we may have reached. For him curiosity was a means of grace. We note from the record that what saddened him about the religious people of his time was not so much their more blatant sins as their total lack of curiosity. They had Moses and the prophets and were sure they knew all the answers. They were not about to open their minds or hearts to any new vision of God or disturbing thought about religion. The stories Jesus told, the parables, were designed to rouse curiosity—that's why they often describe extraordinary behavior and raise a host of questions. But many of his most pious contemporaries didn't want to hear them. They were too shocking; they set people off on dangerous paths. How much better to have all questions about God, about worship, about the right way to live, about the destiny of mankind neatly wrapped up and accepted without question.

As for Jesus himself, it's worth remarking that the only authentic glimpse we have of his own childhood reveals his intense curiosity. His parents, you remember, when they lost him on a visit to Jerusalem, "found him in the temple, sitting in the midst of the doctors, both hearing them, and asking them questions." We read that once, years later, when he was faced with the unresponsiveness of the average devout and moral citizen to his message of the kingdom, he suddenly broke into prayer, saying: "I thank thee, O Father, Lord of heaven and earth, because thou hast hid these things from the wise and prudent, and hast revealed them unto babes." They were hidden from the wise and prudent simply because their religion was static and taken for granted. It was the "babes"—whatever their ages—who still had the spirit of curiosity.

There's something far wrong with the church when we cease to arouse any curiosity among either our own members or the community we live in. For the church represents Jesus Christ on earth; it is so closely identified with him that the New Testament refers to the church as the body of Christ. And Christ is, beyond question, the person about whom more curiosity has been aroused throughout human history. When he was here in the flesh the questions flew thick and fast: "Who is this?" "Where did he get his healing power?" "What does he want to do?" It was this curiosity of all kinds of people, from the beggars to the rulers, that alarmed the upholders of the religious status quo. We find that his disciples were constantly curious about him—never more so than when the report began to circulate that he had risen from the dead. And when the name of Jesus Christ was eventually pronounced in the great cities of the Roman Empire, the questioning spread and all kinds of people—from Greek philosophers to necromancers, from Roman officers to slaves became intensely curious about him.

So it has gone on as the centuries have passed. Continually the church seems to have tamed this curiosity, to have presented a Christ about whom no questions need to be asked. But every now and then an Augustine, a Luther, a Wesley, a Schweitzer would come along, and the questions would break out all over again. We have seen this swing from indifference to curiosity happen again in our own generation. Not so long ago the name of Jesus Christ was only to be heard within the churches—unless it was being used as an oath. And within the churches no one was asking questions; it was assumed that everybody knew who we were talking about. Now there has been a startling change. Suddenly the person of Jesus Christ has become again the object of an intense curiosity. Books are appearing that raise all kinds of questions about him. New theories appear almost every month as to his character and background, and arguments range about his trial and crucifixion and the reports of his resurrection. The younger generation has been fascinated by the image of Christ, whether as a young martyr who was sacrificed by the establishment or as the divine Savior who can bring a release from bondage to the drug scene or a materialist society. Who could have guessed just a few years ago that a musical would arrive on Broadway with the title *Jesus Christ Superstar*? Or that it would be only one of a series of musicals, plays, and movies centering on the person of Christ?

What is going to be the response of the churches to this new curiosity about their Lord? Already some are expressing shock and disapproval. Those who have always placed Jesus securely in the conventional framework of creed and worship resent the startling things that are being said about him in modern books and movies and stage productions. They remind me of the disciple who once protested to Jesus: "Teacher, we saw a man who was driving out demons in your name, and we told him to stop because he doesn't belong to our group." And Jesus' reply was: "Don't try to stop him. . . . Whoever is not against us is for us." It seems to me that Jesus always welcomed genuine curiosity about his person and his work, and that he never insisted on a full understanding before he enlisted a man or woman in his cause. He even set the disciples out on a mission *before* they had given the answer to the great question: "Who do you say that I am?"

It seems to me that the churches should welcome the current lively interest in the person of Christ, just as Paul used to rejoice when Christ was being talked about even by his opponents. He writes to the Philippian church about the great commotion that was going on concerning the gospel that he preached and the numerous movements that were attacking his conception of Christ. "It doesn't matter!" he cries, "I am happy about it—just so Christ is preached in every way possible, whether from right or wrong motives." So those within the churches today should be happy that Christ is being talked about and is no longer a classified topic, held top secret in some ecclesiastical archive. It will do us good, if we are conventional Christians, to be forced to confront new and startling interpretations of the person and life of Christ. We shall be forced to reexamine our understanding and thus to expose ourselves again to the amazing record of the New Testament.

For to welcome the new curiosity about Jesus is by no means to be ready to accept every new proposition that comes along. In fact, the instructed Christian will soon recognize in many of the latest theories about Jesus some very old theories that were examined and rejected by the church more than fifteen hundred years ago. Curious Christians, in the best sense of the term, are not those who fall for every new presentation of Jesus but those who are stimulated by any honest thinking inside or outside the church, and are able to refresh their own image of Christ by a renewed study of the Scripture records.

This leads me to say that the curiosity I am talking about is not a mere "interest" in Christ and in religion in general. The difference between true Christian curiosity and some of the current "interest in religion" is that the curious Christian expects to find some kind of an answer and make some kind of a decision. "Ask, seek, knock" continues to be the program of an active Christian, but he never forgets the promise that is attached to these words. "Ask, *and you will receive;* seek, *and you will find;* knock, *and the door will be opened.* A living church is not a community where religious questions are endlessly debated, but where men and women find their curiosity rewarded and commit their lives to the truth that has been revealed. The curious Christian expects an answer to his queries. He believes, unlike so many modern philosophers, that the universe responds to the kind of questions he is asking about the meaning of life, the destiny of man, and the mystery of his own being. They are not meaningless questions. There is a God who will answer.

Religion comes alive again in any man or woman when they are bold enough to release again the inquisitive spirit they have stifled and really ask about God, really seek for an answer, really knock at some of these long-closed doors. This is the curiosity that Christ promises to reward. "You *will* receive; you *will* find; the door *will* be opened." And the joy of such discovery is that once it is made we realize that there is more to come, right up to the moment of our leaving this mortal life. As I find written on the bottom of the page of certain reports that come to my desk: "More . . . more . . . more." That is the motto of the curious Christian right to the end. He knows that there is "More . . . more . . . more."

3

Unfreezing Your Image of God

In a prisoner-of-war camp where I once spent some time as a guest of the Third Reich, we used to pass a lot of time going to lectures. These were given by our fellow prisoners who happened to be experts on some particular subject, and I remember listening to expositions of such varied topics as bird-watching, the philosophy of Kant, modern economics, mercantile law, Roman history, and the poetry of T. S. Eliot. What mattered to us was not so much the topic—almost any one would do—but the ability of the lecturer to arouse our curiosity and open up a new field of interest. In the early days we flocked to whatever was being offered, but as the years went by, we became a little more discriminating, and the custom grew up of posting a notice on the camp board announcing a forthcoming series of lectures and asking those interested in attending to sign their initials. If one collected a dozen or so signatures, then that was the green light to book a room and start preparing.

One day, in collaboration with my colleague in the camp who was a chaplain of another denomination, I decided to offer a course in Christian apologetics—which is a long-winded way of saying that we were going to try to expound the Christian gospel and persuade others to accept it. Since we had in view atheists and agnostics, as well as the majority who were at least nominally attached to some church, we decided to offer lectures on such topics as "Is God a Myth?" which we duly inscribed on our notice as the theme of the first lecture. As I hovered around the notice board one day to see if we were going to collect an audience, I saw one of our somewhat older inhabitants studying the board with an anxious frown. He turned and saw me. "That's a dangerous thing you're doing," he said. "How do you mean—dangerous?" I asked. "Well," he said, "don't you realize lots of us don't want to start thinking about these things because if we did, we might find that we didn't believe any more?"

That remark shook me, as I am incapable of understanding what satisfaction anyone can get from holding on to a faith that he doesn't believe will stand examination. I tried to explain that the course was designed to show what solid grounds we have for believing, and if it led to anyone's religion being shaken up, then perhaps that was just what was needed. Surely it's the truth that we want, and only a religion that respects truth is worth having. But he wouldn't be convinced and went away muttering, "Dangerous, dangerous."

In the end we got our audience—about half the camp—and we certainly got our debate and religious awakening. But it's this one man's fear that I remember now, for I think that it's typical of quite a number at the present time. They want to remain undisturbed with their religious affiliation, whatever it happens to be, and don't want to be forced to examine the content of their beliefs, for they have a suspicion that it might not stand up to the light of their mature understanding. What happens to so many people is that they naturally acquire their belief in God and their other religious convictions in early childhood. Then, in adolescence they freeze these beliefs in one corner of their minds. In every other department of life they mature. They put away childish things, and they expand their understanding of nature, of literature, of art, of history, and of human relationships. But their religion remains frozen at the childish level, and so, naturally, they are afraid to thaw it out lest what emerges would be totally unacceptable in the light of their mature understanding.

The first thing we have to do if we want a vital faith is to have the courage to unfreeze our image of God, to bring our latent beliefs out into the open. The New Testament gives no encouragement to those who want to retain their religion in a little childish segment of their mind. What Jesus said about the need to become as little children has nothing to do with this refusal to grow up in the faith. The childlike spirit can be retained at any age, and by the most mature and sophisticated people. Jesus would probably have considered that the desire to hang on to a childish religion was one way of hiding our talent in the earth. "I was afraid," said the slothful servant, "and went and hid thy talent in the earth." Jesus looked for disciples who would grow in the faith—mentally, as well as morally and spiritually. And his apostles continually reminded the first Christians of the need to mature. "When I was a child," said Paul, "my speech, my outlook, and my thoughts were all childish. When I grew up I had finished with childish things." The writer to the Hebrews rebukes the Christians he was addressing for wanting milk instead of solid food. "Anyone who lives on milk," he says, "being an infant, does not know what is right. But grown men can take solid food; their perceptions are trained by long use to discriminate between good and evil."

What happens when we do have the curiosity to examine the religion we have been clinging to?

There is, of course, the danger that it looks so childish we feel like throwing it all out of the window. I remember a fellow student once saying to me when I asked why he had given up the Christian activities in which we shared: "Well, when I was growing up, I began to have doubts. And whenever a doubt came along I put it on the shelf. Then one day, when I had a look, all the doubts fell off the shelf and there was nothing left." Nothing could more clearly reveal the folly of refusing to let one's religion grow with the expanding mind. But I would plead with any who have had, or are having, this experience, to remember that religion should not be judged by our childish memories, and also that these memories should not be despised. If we have the patience to begin again, building on the fragments of religion that remain to us, we can have the excitement of discovering what faith can mean in the context of our life and our outlook today.

Instead of throwing away the remnants of our belief in God, we might begin to ask what men and women of this modern world have found to be a satisfying and illuminating religion. Before we decide that all kinds of faith are mere delusion, we might, for instance, listen to the testimony of Albert Einstein, who shaped so much of the scientific age in which we live. "The most beautiful thing we can experience," he wrote, "is the mysterious. It is the source of all true art and science. He

37

to whom this emotion is a stranger, who can no longer pause to wonder and stand rapt in awe, is as good as dead: his eyes are closed. This insight into the mystery of life, coupled though it be with fear, has also given rise to religion. To know that what is impenetrable to us really exists, manifesting itself as the highest wisdom and the most radiant beauty which our dull faculties can comprehend only in their most primitive forms—this knowledge, this feeling, is at the center of true religiousness. In this sense and in this sense only, I belong in the ranks of devoutly religious men."

So let's unfreeze our image of God without any fear that we're going to say good-bye to any kind of religion. What happens when we ask ourselves what picture we have of the power behind the universe, the One to whom we have all at some time addressed our prayers? I feel sure that if a hundred of us tried to express publicly the nature of the God we believe in, no two would say exactly the same thing. The answers would range from very concrete conceptions of a kind of invisible superman to the vaguest statements about an impersonal life-force. Some might say: "He's like my kindly old grandfather"; others that they think of an invisible power like electricity. Few people would feel satisfied with what they said for the very good reason that God must be infinite—and obviously the infinite cannot be defined. *"Le Dieu défini est le Dieu fini,"* the French say—"God defined is God finished."

Now I wouldn't have the temerity to guess what *your* image of God is right now. And it is certainly not my business to try to replace it by mine. But, in the light of what the Bible says, and in the light of what we know of the person and teaching of Jesus Christ, I'm going to suggest that there are some discoveries awaiting us all—if we have the curiosity to look. The Bible refrain "Seek ye the Lord" is surely among other things an invitation to enlarge and to deepen our image of God.

Let me suggest two discoveries we may make as we unfreeze our image and open our minds and our imagination to the Spirit of God.

For many of us the revelation will come in words which I borrow from the title of a stimulating book by J. B. Phillips—*Your God Is Too Small.* In spite of the fact that the Bible keeps reiterating the ineffable glory of God—"My thoughts are not your thoughts, neither are your ways my ways, saith the Lord. For as the heavens are higher than the earth, so are my ways higher than your ways, and my thoughts than your thoughts," we read in the Old Testament, and in the New, "O the depth of the riches both of the wisdom and knowledge of God! how unsearchable are his judgments, and his ways past finding out!" —in spite of the consant reminder that God's being is vast enough to include everything that man

39

has ever, or will ever, discover, we keep limiting him within the narrow limits of our own experience.

We limit him very crudely by our tendency to think of him as sharing our narrow background of race and language. For Anglo-Saxons his image tends to be white and Protestant, and his language, of course, English. No matter how often we sing:

> Join hands, then, brothers of the faith,
>   Whate'er your race may be!
> Who serves my Father as a son
>   Is surely kin to me,

we still cling subconsciously to the notion that somehow he is "one of us," that he is confined by our culture, our outlook, and—worst of all—our prejudices. Only thus can we account for the deplorable fact that religious people have often demonstrated the worst kind of racial bigotry. Their God is too small, crushed into the narrow framework of their own little empire of prejudice and fear.

Then, we are all tempted to limit our idea of God by confining him to the religious sector of life. What I mean is that we easily form the habit of thinking that God is chiefly concerned with our prayers, with churches, with questions of right and wrong. He is the president of the religious department, much busier—if I can put it this way—on

Sundays than on Mondays. Just as we may find it difficult to believe that he is as interested in a Chinese communist as an American Christian, so we may not realize that he is as concerned with Wall Street as with the Vatican. If we check up on the Bible we'll find perhaps to our surprise that there is no religious department at all. God is there seen as active everywhere—the Lord of all human life, personal and social. Everything—politics, economics, public health, architecture, recreation—is related to him.

Now that our minds are being stretched to contemplate an immense universe in which this earth is less than a speck of dust in a huge cathedral, many are wondering if the God of our fathers is big enough to believe in today. And when Christians talk as if God's sole concern is with this fraction of creation and this particular creature we call man, it is no wonder that the modern world says: "Your God is too small." But the Bible books, in spite of being written before the discoveries of modern astronomy, witness to a God who is Creator and Lord of everything that is. If there should in fact be intelligent beings elsewhere in the universe, he is their God too. "To whom then will ye liken me, or shall I be equal? saith the Holy One. Lift up your eyes on high, and behold who created these things, that bringeth out their host by number." (Isaiah 40:25.) There is no discovery yet to be made that can eliminate the image of this God,

41

the One whose infinite creative power and mysterious purpose is far beyond the grasp of our minds or the sweep of our imagination.

But if in many ways our God is too small, can it not also be said that our God is also too vague? You may have been thinking, as I quoted the Bible on the transcendent, all-embracing glory of God, that I could also have cited many passages where God is spoken of in very familiar, all-too-human terms. This is perfectly true, and we shall find this aspect of the Bible equally fascinating as we unfreeze our image of God. If it is possible for us to limit our God by restricting his concerns to the little area of human religion on this planet, it is equally possible to limit him by denying that he can be personally concerned with each one of us, by having such a vague image of him that he is not One with whom we can have an intimate relationship. Nothing is more paralyzing for religion than a concept of God that denies him any of the qualities that make us truly human. A God who cannot think, or plan, or care, or love, or laugh is surely something less than the men and women he has brought into being. Yet there is a popular notion that the only image of God an intelligent person can have today is one that is vague, inanimate, impersonal.

To unfreeze our image of God is to allow for a new understanding of how we can really know and trust this infinite Lord of all being. This is what the Bible calls the "good news." For if there is one thing that Jesus Christ makes clear, it is that you and I can commune with God as directly and confidently as a child with his father. The God he reveals is big enough to be able to care for the least of his creatures. That is the theme of so much of what Jesus said. But the New Testament goes even further. Those who are curious enough to start thinking again about what they once learned about what is called "the divinity of Christ" will find that the doctrine could also be called "the humanity of God." For when we read that Jesus said: "He that hath seen me hath seen the Father," he is giving the startling good news that everything we see in him—goodness, honesty, kindness, holiness, and infinite love—is to be found in God. To those who begin to glimpse this truth the process of unfreezing their image of God becomes more and more exciting and life-giving. For the figure that emerges as the Lord of all being shines with the humanity of Christ.

4

The Fascination of Jesus

Recently I've noticed a new name appearing on buttons, on posters, on balloons, and among the scribbles on subway walls. It's the name of Jesus. An old name, perhaps, but the content is new. For this is not the work of old-fashioned evangelists or of the few religious enthusiasts who have for years carried their placards through crowded streets. It's all part of the youth movement. Somehow a whole new generation seems to be discovering Jesus.

Every one of us will react to this phenomenon according to our prejudices. Some will scoff and dismiss the whole thing as "the latest fad." Some will interpret the movement as an inevitable swing of the pendulum for a generation that has been religiously undernourished. Some will joyfully claim that once again a real Christian revival is under way. And others will cautiously analyze the movement and ask how solid are the foundations and how serious the commitment to the living Christ. I am not about to line up with any of these judgments today—it's too soon anyway; I am simply glad that this generation has at least the curiosity to ask the inevitable questions about Jesus.

For this is what I find hardest to understand about many of my own contemporaries. I can understand a man or woman being an atheist, or an agnostic. I can understand someone who says he has studied the New Testament and is unwilling to accept what it says about Jesus. What strikes me as almost incomprehensible is that an intelligent man or woman raised in the Western world should have no curiosity whatever about this man whose impact on our civilization has been so enormous and about whom such staggering claims are made.

I suppose it has something to do with what you might call inoculation. Just as by being inoculated with a small dose of smallpox we are made immune to the disease, lots of people are given an inoculation of the Christian gospel. I dimly remember as a very small child getting the ceremonies of vaccination and baptism rather mixed up—and perhaps I wasn't all that wrong. I don't mean for a moment to question the value of the sacrament of baptism, but isn't it true that for many in recent generations there has been a brief exposure in

45

childhood to the gospel of Christ, which is followed by a lapse into a kind of shadowy background religion? It's taken for granted that everyone knows who Jesus is, what his gospel is, and what the Bible is about. So it is much easier to arouse excitement about any of these things among people who have scarcely heard of them. Perhaps many among the "Jesus movement" today are boys and girls who never learned anything at all about Christianity at home or school, and it hits them with its pristine power. Older people who show little or no live interest in the person of Christ probably feel that it's all just part of a religious tradition that needn't be investigated any more.

Fortunately it's never too late for anyone to get curious again about Jesus and to begin to read the Bible with new eyes. I've seen it happen to men and women of all ages. Suddenly they find themselves asking new questions—or perhaps very old ones that come alive again for them. They come to church or to some lectures with a new curiosity. They begin to discover that they had really only a minimal knowledge of Jesus and the vaguest idea of the contents of the New Testament. They take the risk of exposing themselves to all sorts of ideas—some helpful, some startling, some very disturbing—and so join the company of those who, in the words of Jesus himself, ask, seek, and knock. And so, in God's time, they are given, they find, and the doors are opened.

When you come to think of it, there is no more astonishing fact in human history than the impact of a young Jewish preacher, who was executed by the Romans long ago, upon almost the entire human race to this very day. Even a generation that lacks respect for history is compelled to date its letters by counting from the supposed year of his birth. The amazing story of the Jewish people from whom he came is enough to arouse our curiosity, and the story of this one brief life raises questions that demand some kind of answer. When you add to this the fact that millions of his followers to the present day think of his death by crucifixion as something much more than martyrdom and go on to claim that it was followed by a resurrection, you have still more to arouse any questioning mind. Remove any reference to these beliefs from the art and literature of the Western world and what would be left? Even if today we are watching the emergence of a secular culture that seems innocent of any knowledge of Jesus, can anyone say that his image has vanished and that now he can be safely forgotten? He continues to fascinate each new generation in a different way, and we are beginning to realize that he is not tied to what we call our Western civilization. Even as many turn their backs on him here, he is being discovered afresh in Africa and the Far East.

There are two directions in which we can look when our curiosity is aroused about Jesus Christ.

One is the Bible within which we find the story of his origins, a brief account of his life, some extracts from his teaching, a witness to his death and resurrection, and an account of the impact he made on the first of his followers. The other is the church, the strange community so difficult to define, but somehow constantly *there,* in every generation, uniting all kinds of people in a unique kind of loyalty to Jesus and communion with him. The church, once you have stopped thinking of it as a rather faded and familiar institution, should arouse your curiosity. When you think of its diversity, its frailty, its many betrayals of the spirit of Jesus, its vulnerability to attack in every century, you find yourself wondering how it can possibly still be around. And curiosity about the church can well lead you to some startling discoveries about the presence of Christ in worship, in sacrament, and in service to humanity.

But it is the Bible, and especially the New Testament, that offers us the historic evidence about Jesus; and when we turn to it afresh our fascination with Jesus is bound to increase. If, for example, we take one of the Gospels in a modern translation, and read it straight through as we would any other book, we may meet with a Jesus who is not altogether the same as we had vaguely supposed him to be. For the image of Jesus is often built up in our minds by the selected snippets from the Gospels we hear read or quoted. Only a wide-awake reading of the whole story allows him, as it were, to make a total impression on our hearts and minds. And what an impression it is!

Here is one who seems to have surprised and astonished everyone who met him, and yet remained entirely loyal to the highest religious traditions of his people. He had a way of taking accepted truths like the fatherhood of God and making them blaze with new meaning. He quoted the Bible constantly, but on his lips the words seemed to stab like a sword and turn life upside down. He was passionately on the side of the poor and the oppressed but took no part in the movements of militant revolution. His teaching was so simple that children understood him, yet so demanding that even his disciples thought it impossible to follow. No one was ever more down to earth in relating religion to the practical decisions of daily life, yet he could see the heavens opening and seemed equally at home in that transcendent world of God. He spoke as if the whole of humanity was his parish, laying claim to the love and loyalty of all mankind, yet he lived and died within the limits of a little nation, completely identified with the language and culture, the hopes and fears, and the religious imagery and traditions of the Jewish people. He apparently loved the solitude of the hills and lakes, but gave himself voluntarily to the crowds in the throbbing and threatening communities of town and city. He could speak to a nation, be moved to compassion by a crowd, and weep over a city. But the most astonishing part of the story is his complete concentration on one single human being without any regard for those labels and masks which distort our judgment still today. A religious dignitary, a Roman officer, a peasant girl, a fisherman, a Samaritan woman, a scholar, a blind beggar—for him the labels didn't exist. Each one was a potential child of God; for each one he cared, and cared differently; and for each one he had something to give. And each of them was fascinated—attracted or repelled by what he said and did.

He was gentle—but could be immensely stern and threatening. He was patient—but constantly warned that the time was short. He seemed to have unbounded hope in what God's grace can do for even the most degraded human being, but was utterly realistic about the power of evil in the human heart. He foresaw no rosy future for his followers and was no blind optimist about the way ahead for the human race; yet he talked with complete confidence of the victory of love and the final triumph of the kingdom of God.

It is not surprising, then, that his contemporaries, and millions since across the world, couldn't help asking: "Who is this?" Alone among the religious leaders he made the question of his own person and mission absolutely central. "Who do they say I am?" "Who do *you* say I am?" This is what fascinates all who have the curiosity to read this story, all who are again being confronted with the presence of this Jesus in our modern world. For the central enigma of the story is that somehow Jesus steps across the boundary of our human limitations. In the Gospels we find the sudden flash that transfigures the intense humanity of Jesus and lets us see the presence of our God. The rest of the New Testament makes it very clear that his first followers didn't just follow the example and teaching of a great prophet but knew the presence and the healing power of the Son of God—God incarnate among us.

This also is inescapably in the new agitation about the person of Jesus. It is not only the figure of the man who demonstrated the power of love, or who tore the pretenses of conventional morality away, or who defied the hypocrisies of the self-righteous and the callous that fascinates a new generation. It is the glimpse of God in him, the realization that there is still to be found in him a transforming and liberating power, and a hope and meaning for our human lives today that makes those young men and women of the hippie generation raise an arm with finger pointed upward as a sign of their newfound hope. Jesus fascinates because in him we find a window through which we can look beyond the frustrations and flatness of a merely secular culture; because in him we find a divine source of healing and of hope.

51

"Who am I?" asks Jesus. That once again is the question that is emerging, after all our debates about God, our endless efforts to make Christianity relevant—as they say—to the modern world. And the question needs to be answered again, even by those who think that they disposed of it fifty years ago. For who can claim to have reached what Paul called "the measure of the stature of the fulness of Christ"? Today there are facets of the gospel that are gleaming again with a new and surprising light. The Christ who fascinates is not only the unforgettable teacher of Galilee, not only the Son of God who died for the sins of men. He is . . . the cosmic Christ to whom all things move, the Lord of the future who gives meaning and fulfillment to the anguish and aspiration of the human tale amid the silent mysteries of the ongoing universe.

Teilhard de Chardin, the brilliant scientist, theologian, and philosopher whose life was given to a study of the evolution of life and the structure of the universe as disclosed by modern science, has delighted some and irritated others by his fusion of scientific and religious insights. Once again what has fascinated many in his writings has been his vision of the convergence of all things in Christ. He writes:

The whole world is concentrated and uplifted in expectancy of union with the divine; yet at the same time it encounters an insurmountable barrier. For nothing can come to Christ unless he himself takes it and gathers it unto himself. Towards Christ all the immortal monads converge. Not a single atom, however lowly or imperfect, but must cooperate—at least by way of repulsion and reflexion—in the fulfillings of Christ. . . . The universe takes on the lineaments of Jesus; but then there is great mystery: for he who thus becomes discernible is Jesus crucified. Christ is love as a person; he compels recognition as a world.

For those who confess themselves baffled by this kind of thinking, and perhaps discouraged by the immensity of the whole subject, let me close with a quotation from another very great man of this century. Probably nobody has ever devoted so much time and study to the person of Christ and the lives of him that have been written over the years as Albert Schweitzer. As a young man his study in the seminary at Strasbourg was crammed from floor to ceiling with books about Jesus in German, French, and English. When he read them all, he wrote his *Quest of the Historical Jesus,* which startled a whole generation and set off arguments that are not yet ended. Yet in spite of the confusions of interpretations and his vast knowledge of the intricacies of the subject, he was able to write in this simple passage at the end of the book in which he explains the essence of the fascination that Jesus had for him:

He comes to us as One unknown, without a name, as of old, by the lake-side. He came to those men who knew him not. He speaks to us the same word: "Follow thou me!" and sets us to the tasks which he has to fulfill for our time. He commands. And to those who obey, whether they be wise or simple, he will reveal himself in the toils, the conflicts, the sufferings which they shall pass through in his fellowship, and, as an ineffable mystery, they shall learn in their own experience who he is.

Fascinated? Yes; but it is through obedience that we shall know.

5

Beyond Death - Are You Curious?

These words from the book of Job summarize in the form of a simple question the essence of the great debate about the afterlife. When preachers, philosophers, poets, mystics, scientists, and psychiatrists have said their say, and we have listened to every kind of interpretation of what is called "eternal life," this is the question to which the ordinary man or woman returns: "If a man die, shall he live again?" It may be that there are many today who have been so conditioned by their secular or Marxist upbringing that the question is quickly brushed off with a contemptuous "No," but it's hard to believe that there is anyone at all who has not had even a flicker of curiosity about the almost universal human belief that there is something for us beyond the grave. Can anyone really experience the death of someone close to them or contemplate their own without at least an echo of this question crossing his mind: "If a man die, shall he live again?" Does this life snuff out like a candle—and that's that?

I find it fascinating that this topic should be raised right in the middle of the Bible in the form of a question. Those who are not familiar with the Scriptures are apt to think that they are full of information about heaven and hell. The mere fact that it's called a "Holy Book" suggests to them that it deals almost entirely with another world. The fact is that you can read far into the Bible without finding any reference at all to an after-life. It is only when the writers began to worry about such questions as the unfairness of human life—the way the wicked often seem to prosper while the good are oppressed—that they envisaged the possibility of another life where justice would be perfectly done. It was when they began to understand how unique and precious is the life of an individual human being that they found it hard to believe that physical death means its total annihilation. So the thought of immortality first arises in the Bible as a wistful question, a question that is echoed in every society on earth and in every age right to the present: "If a man die, shall he live again?"

The Bible, then, approaches this topic by arousing our curiosity rather than by beating us over the head with a lot of dogmatic data about eternal life. And I should like to follow its example as I talk about what may lie beyond death. First come our questions, real questions, serious questions; and then we are ready to listen for an answer. As you read on through the Bible you can hear that answer coming; you can hear it louder and louder as you reach the New Testament, and when you come to the close of the book of Revelation you will be left with one triumphant word ringing in your ears—resurrection—and the simple affirmation that because he lives we shall live also.

I'm not going to pretend that I have any other answer than this, but I don't reach it without hearing the questions in my own heart and mind. I don't proclaim it simply because it is part of a series of propositions drilled into me at seminary. Often when conducting a funeral service I feel the eyes of the bereaved upon me as if they were saying: "Yes, we know what the book says; we know that you are expected to use these prayers, and make these statements—but do you, personally, really believe it?" Sometimes, at home, or in a car returning from the graveside, the question will come right out. And the answer is "Yes"; but a "Yes" that has reached me, and gripped me, from the mists of a hundred questions. It is not an automatic response, but an echo of a divine "Yes" that I have heard through the agony and victory of Christ.

57

"If a man die, shall he live again?" It is only those who are curious enough to ask the question who can possibly know any answer. And it is better to be curious right now than to wait until the question springs upon us in a moment of crisis. The trouble is that, for some time now, we have lived in a world that has discouraged us from asking any such question. In this period of immense concentration on material progress, of spectacular achievement in the physical universe, of vast hopes and fears bounded by the secular world of here and now, it has not been easy to contemplate the eternal. We have been, to a great extent, an orphan generation—cut off, as it were, horizontally from our ancestors and vertically from the sense of the transcendent and divine. It has not been a time for either history or theology to flourish in the popular mind. Just as there has been little live contact with our ancestors, so there has been even less with the world invisible.

There is little in a modern city like New York or Los Angeles to encourage belief in any other world than that of skyscrapers and automobiles. The very names remind us of how far we have come from the days when everybody lived under the sign of the eternal and invisible. For old York in England was a town that nestled under the shadow of the mighty minster whose soaring towers pointed to heaven and whose glistening windows reminded the citizens of the world to come. And Los Angeles—the Angels—speaks of what was very real to its founders. Who would name a city today for the angelic hosts of heaven? In the sixteenth century the thought of death and what lies beyond was never far away. A poet could sing of his ladylove or the beauties of nature, but the thought of mortality was never far away. *"Timor mortis conturbat me,"* they sang—"The fear of death disturbs me." A businessman in those days would probably have had a skull on his desk rather than a photograph of his wife. Shakespeare's characters could never shake off the thought of life after death.

Hamlet, contemplating suicide, is held by a curious, troubling thought about what happens next:

> To die, to sleep;
> To sleep: perchance to dream: ay, there's the rub;
> For in that sleep of death what dreams may come
> When we have shuffled off this mortal coil,
> Must give us pause.

But it's not only the Hamlets, the ruminating, introspective characters, who brood on the future life. Even the villains act in the consciousness of a judgment to come—if only to defy it. Macbeth plotting murder mutters to himself:

> That but this blow
> Might be the be-all and the end-all here,

> But here, upon this bank and shoal of time,
> We'd jump the life to come.

There's not the same atmosphere of eternity about our modern literature on the whole. It reflects the life of the concrete canyons and the neat suburban home where the only reminder of mortality is the discreet obituary in the morning paper. Death has been smoothed away, and in some quarters is the only unmentionable subject left in these outspoken times. For a long time we have lived in this climate of secularism with little to remind us of a world unseen and without the backdrop of eternity.

Yet now we can see a whole generation having second thoughts. Not many are so confident that the line of human progress runs toward a total concentration on the material and the present moment. There is, in fact, no steady movement in history from total concentration on life after death to a complete dismissal of the subject. In New Testament times, for instance, there was far less confidence in immortality than five hundred years later. So the inquisitive mind is bound to ask if the period we have just lived through was right in ignoring so completely the thought of an afterlife. Does it really look as if men and women were on the move to a freer, more fulfilling, more joyful life the more they rid themselves of any thought of a life to come? Was the period of concentration on the visible and material really a time of human advance and liberation? The answer is so obvious that it is not surprising that we are now witnessing a new quest for the world invisible, for the values of the spirit, and even for some assurance of life after death.

This new curiosity is taking many forms—from the rediscovery of the radiant hope that speaks again in the pages of the New Testament to the investigation of the psychic realm of spiritism and the occult. Everything points to a revulsion from the materialism that ruled out the dimension of eternity and thought the question: "If a man die, shall he live again" a mere waste of time. Few are so certain any more that our artificial, mechanized, computerized, metropolitan existence is telling us the real truth about our human life. This dawned on me once when I returned to New York from a vacation spent visiting an island off the coast of Scotland where one is near to the skies, the mountains, and the sea, where the past seems as close as the present, and where I had listened to strange tales from the world invisible. The cultural shock of landing in a huge city immediately afterward left me at first wondering if I had been in some unreal, crazy place—until I began to think. Where, after all, is one likely to be nearer to the truth? Which is really the crazy place—the little island where men have lived and died in the confidence of another world to come or the frantic, sprawling city where we live at some distance from the realities of the soil and the sky, deafened by our own noise and blinded by the artifacts of an affluent society? I have heard the island of Iona described as a "thin place"—meaning that veil between this life and the eternal is so tenuous that you can say with Francis Thomson:

> O world invisible, we view thee,
> O world intangible, we touch thee,
> O world unknowable, we know thee,
> Incomprehensible, we clutch thee!

I would like to have such a grasp on life eternal that every place, even the modern city, could be for me a "thin place." Isn't that where our new curiosity is leading us?

But how do we find our way among all the competing voices that offer directions about life after death? Let me offer some guidelines that have helped me in this quest.

1. We should beware of those who claim to know too much. Books and pamphlets cross my desk which offer detailed descriptions of life beyond the grave, telling just how many will be in heaven and who will be in hell; offering timetables of events to come or details about the activities of the afterlife. I was warned long ago that when talking about life after death the preacher should be confident in his declaration of the promise of

the gospel but very reticent in his speculations about the nature of eternal life—what Reinhold Niebuhr used to call "the furniture of heaven and the temperature of hell." We are no more able to envisage the real conditions of life there than we can explain what we mean by red, blue, and green to one who was born color-blind. For many of the questions that arouse our curiosity, a veil of agnosticism is a better garment for the preacher than the mantle of the pundit.

2. And that leads me to another guideline—the realization that there is a wrong kind of curiosity in these matters. While it is surely natural and right for all of us to ask the fundamental question: "If a man die, shall he live again?" and hope for a convincing answer, we waste our time when we persist in asking how. Here again the Bible is a sure guide. You will find that Jesus spoke and lived in the absolutely certain conviction that there is a life beyond the grave but refused to give any details of its nature. When speaking of his own death and what lay beyond, he said "Where I am you may be also." That was all. On one occasion when he was pressed to say more about conditions in the resurrection life, he just said, "You will be like the angels," knowing full well that we have no means of knowing just how the angels are. The trouble with excessive curiosity about the next life is that it leads to a preoccupation with questions that cannot be answered now,

63

to a desire for material proofs of a spiritual world, and to a neglect of the major truth that we should so order our lives now as to be ready for an eternal communion with our God.

3. For this is the great guideline in all such questions. Our conviction about the reality of life after death comes to us, and grows in us, as we relate to our God here and now. The only definition of eternal life I know in the Bible is "knowing God." Quite simply, my belief in life beyond death rests on the fact that to know him now is to know him forever. To put it another way: when God grasps you he does not let go—not even when the body wears out and the heart stops beating. For the Christian no other assurance is needed. If our curiosity leads us to the God who shines upon us the light of his crucified and risen Son, we shall need no more assurance about the life beyond. "In my Father's house are many rooms; if it were not so, would I have told you that I go to prepare a place for you?" (John 14:2 RSV.) That's all we need—but it would be good to die still curious about these rooms in the Father's house.

6

Holy Spirit in Hiding

There are few subjects on which the average Christian layman would be less willing to express his convictions than that of the Holy Spirit. The word "God" is generally understood no matter how varied our images of him may be. The word "Jesus" means something fairly definite in spite of our differences as to his person and his significance in the human story. But the words "Holy Spirit"—and still more "Holy Ghost"—induce a feeling of hazy helplessness, even of boredom. We all know that the words complete the familiar doxology: "Glory be to the Father, and to the Son, and to the Holy Ghost," but few could explain just why there has to be this third expression of our faith in the triune God.

Sermons and church literature abound in references to the Father God and to Jesus Christ, but the Spirit is mentioned only in a few vague phrases about the "guidance," the "leading," or the "in-dwelling" of the Spirit of God. How often have you heard a sermon on this topic? How many books or pamphlets do you remember that deal with the Holy Spirit? Does the festival of Pentecost, which commemorates the coming of the Spirit on the disciples and the birth of the Christian church, play a large part in the celebrations of your local church? Or would it be true to say that, compared with the excitement of Christmas and Easter, it comes and goes almost without notice? I sometimes think that in many places today the situation is not unlike that in Ephesus long ago when the apostle Paul asked a group of professing Christians: "Did you receive the Holy Spirit when you became believers?" and received the reply: "No, we have not even heard that there *is* a Holy Spirit."

Outside the church I imagine there are few who ever give much thought to the subject except insofar as "Spirit of God" looks like a conveniently vague expression that doesn't raise awkward questions about a personal divinity. Whereas from time to time questions of Christian doctrine spill over into popular controversy, few will have heard of any excitement concerning the Holy Ghost. (Incidentally, the very use of the word "ghost," which is a carry-over from Elizabethan usage when it meant simply "spirit," has helped to increase the sense of vagueness, or even spookiness, in the popular mind.) This part of the church's teaching seems to belong to some hidden message. At any rate, the church seems to have kept the Spirit in hiding.

Yet there is something in this bewilderment and indifference that ought to arouse our curiosity. Here is a central theme of the Christian message, to be found in all the creeds and confessions, expressed in a thousand hymns, and clearly derived from what the Bible says—and yet few seem to have any idea of what it is all about. Why this confusion? Why this silence? Is there any connection between the hiding of this doctrine and the powerlessness of a great deal of our church life today? Our curiosity will be whetted when we discover that the Bible constantly declares that the vitality of a Christian or a church has to do with the realization of the presence and power of the Holy Spirit. The Risen Christ is said to have promised the disciples: "You will receive power when the Holy Spirit comes upon you." Paul writes: "Where the Spirit of the Lord is, there is liberty," and constantly refers to "the Spirit of Life." The Nicene Creed refers to the Spirit as "the Lord and Giver of life." All this suggests that the "hidden" doctrine might be just what we need. Isn't it worth exploring?

There are one or two straws in the wind today that might rouse our curiosity still more on the subject of the Holy Spirit. One, for instance, is the fact that the fastest growing segment of the Christian church in the last ten years has been that of the churches which go by the name "Pentecostal." These are churches of fairly recent origin, and as the name implies, they claim to have recovered the gifts of the Spirit that were bestowed at Pentecost, including miraculous healings and speaking with tongues. From being a relatively small group they have now spread to what amounts to a denomination of tens of thousands of members, and are represented in the World Council of Churches. Whatever our opinion about their specific doctrines and practices, we must be struck by the fact that such churches with their emphasis on the person and work of the Spirit should be making such an impact across the world today.

Then I am reminded of Karl Barth, the greatest theologian of our time, who said before he died that he believed the most important theme for modern theology was the doctrine of the Holy Spirit. There are signs that he was not alone in this judgment, and both Protestant and Catholic churches are turning their attention in this direction.

Again, I sense in the air today a curious reaching for the kind of religious experience that has in the past been associated with the works and the gifts of the Spirit. What I refer to is the manifest desire for a warm, sustaining, and exciting faith that is something much more than either a cold assent to orthodox doctrines or a feverish running after good causes and good works. People seem to be ready for a religion that works from within, that transcends the old barriers of denominations, that offers a spiritual power beyond the resources of this secular world, that expresses itself with much more freedom and joy than we are accustomed to in the average church. Could it not be that the hidden doctrine, the neglected topic, the forgotten aspect of the Christian gospel is just what we need to be aware of again?

The difficulty about what I am trying to do now is that this power and presence, this agent of life and inner strength, cannot be described in words. It's rather like what happens when one is deeply in love—you can pour out words, as lovers often do, but you know that the essence of the experience is indescribable. Yet it is tremendously real and precious. To talk about the Holy Spirit seems equally futile. To talk too much and try to present a neat and tidy doctrine that all can understand may even be a way of avoiding the living encounter that is the essence of what the Spirit means. I don't expect to argue anyone into a conviction about the person and work of the Holy Spirit. Rather would I pray that through some passing word or mind-picture, through an irrelevant thought that passes through your mind, through a sudden silence perhaps, you might know the inner

presence and power that is the God and Holy
Spirit laying hold upon your life.

Jesus is quoted as saying to Nicodemus: "The
wind blows where it wills, and you hear the sound
of it, but you do not know whence it comes or
whither it goes; so with every one who is born
of the Spirit" (John 3:8 RSV). That sudden sense
of God's reality and his grasp upon you; that opening of a window into a divine dimension; that
stirring of unexpected hope for a better life; that
awareness of what it really means to be accepted
by God here and now, for Christ's sake, without
waiting to justify ourselves or clear our guilt—all
this is the Spirit blowing like the wind: unseen,
unpredictable, but with power to change the shape
of our lives. We cannot command the actions of the
Spirit—but we can be ready: we can hoist our sail
so that something happens when the wind begins
to blow. That is why I am stressing the importance
of the lively and inquiring mind, the genuine kind
of curiosity that opens our lives to the invasion of
this Holy Spirit.

If I *were* to try to put into words what I mean
by the Holy Spirit, to suggest at least some way of
thinking that could explain why Christians have
felt the need to talk about God as Father, Son,
and Holy Ghost, I should say something like this.
"We believe in one God. But this God reveals himself in the Bible and in Christian experience as the
Father and Creator who is *everywhere and always;*

in Jesus Christ, his perfect reflection in human form, who was *there and then,* a historical figure who lived in Palestine two thousand years ago; and through the Holy Spirit who is God in action *here and now.*" I offer this, not as any kind of adequate exposition of the doctrine of the Trinity, but as a way of thinking that I have myself found helpful.

The Holy Spirit is God at work *here and now.* We can have a dim thought of the almighty Creator, Maker of heaven and earth, without it having much effect upon our lives from day to day. Among the 97 percent who—so the statistic goes—profess to believe in God in this country today, there must be many for whom this belief is more a vague background conviction than a living force. Among the millions who would profess to admire Jesus Christ, and to try in some way to follow his teachings, there must be many for whom he is not the living Lord who is a personal companion and force in their lives today. It is the Holy Spirit who brings life to these convictions, who is God speaking to us here and now, God at work in our modern world, God making distant beliefs about a Christ a real and life-changing power.

How curious it is that the Holy Spirit should be for many Christians today a particularly vague and even dull item of belief. For everywhere in the Bible you will find the Spirit mentioned in connection with intense conviction, vitality, and in-

71

vigoration. Some of the most exciting passages in these books are those that describe the action of the Spirit in the life of men and nations. I think of the prophet Ezekiel's vision of the valley of dry bones. It's a fascinating passage in which he pictures the desolation of a people for whom religion has gone dead. "The hand of the Lord was upon me, and carried me out in the spirit of the Lord, and set me down in the midst of the valley which was full of bones. . . . And he said unto me, son of man, can these bones live? And I answered, O Lord God, thou knowest." And the vision ends with this tremendous affirmation of the action of the Spirit of God here and now. "Then he said unto me, Prophesy unto the wind, prophesy, son of man, and say to the wind, Thus saith the Lord God; Come from the four winds, O breath, and breathe upon these slain, that they may live. So I prophesied as he commanded me, and the breath came into them, and they lived, and stood upon their feet, an exceeding great army."

In the New Testament it is the Spirit who not only animates the life and ministry of Jesus but who comes sweeping in like wind and fire to transform his bewildered and dispirited followers into the most dynamic and courageous group of believers the world has ever seen. It is the Spirit who constantly drives them out onto new paths. It is the Spirit who empowers them to challenge the reigning powers of this world and the demonic forces that enslave mankind. It is the Spirit who binds a heterogeneous company of men and women into a fellowship held together with a new kind of love. And it is the Spirit who sheds on them the gifts that we still so desperately need. "The harvest of the Spirit," said Paul, "is love, joy, peace, patience, kindness, goodness, fidelity, gentleness, and self-control." Can anyone think that such things are irrelevant and obscure, with no application to your life and mine today?

For those first Christians the Spirit was always the life-giver. The Bible is just one collection of human literature among many others, until the Spirit comes into action. But then it is God here and now lighting up these pages so that in them we hear him speak, and from them the figure of Jesus walks out alive and challenging. In the same way a sermon is just a kind of spoken essay, a religious editorial, a psychological, pep talk, or a series of warmed-up Christian clichés, unless and until the Holy Spirit takes hold, and the Word of the living God comes through to us. In the same way the water of baptism, the bread and wine of Holy Communion, remain just that—water, bread, and wine—except for the life-giving action of the Holy Spirit, God here and now transforming them into the living channels of his grace.

Perhaps, after all, there is a sense in which the Holy Spirit must remain in hiding, must be beyond our understanding, must be the mysterious hidden power through whom we reach our deepest convictions, and by whose secret operation we are enabled to grow into the image of Christ. The New Testament tells us that the Spirit does not draw attention to himself but points to Jesus and reveals his mind. There are these striking words in the Fourth Gospel: "He will glorify me, for he will take what is mine and declare it to you" (John 16:14 RSV). And the Christian life is constantly described by the apostles as the working of the Spirit from within. The qualities of love and joy and peace are now set out as ideals we must strive to reach, still less as virtues of which we can boast. They are the result of the hidden operation of the Spirit and appear as effortlessly and unselfconsciously as the apples appear on the tree. That is why such qualities are called, not the achievements of a Christian, but the fruit of the Spirit.

If anything I have said here has made the doctrine of the Spirit any more alive and clear for you, I shall be glad. But if it hasn't, I shall not be disappointed. For the Spirit is here not to be talked about but to be responded to. He is here, now, and there are a hundred ways in which he is opening up for us a window into that world where God is near and Christ is forever alive.

7

Discovering the Christian Gospel

Let's suppose that you were whisked away today in a jet plane and found yourself tomorrow in an Indian village on the edge of a jungle. You've rested a little to let your soul catch up with your body, and then you decide to take a little walk. A path leads through the trees toward the next village, and you saunter along absorbing the scenery, wondering perhaps what snakes or wild animals might lurk in the forest. Suddenly you see a man coming toward you. He is barefoot, very simply dressed, and carrying a little bowl. He smiles as you meet and indicates that he can speak English and would like to have a chat. So you sit down on a convenient log and begin to talk.

You soon discover that he is a seeker, one of those familiar figures in the East—a kind of "holy man" who wanders from place to place in quest of spiritual enlightenment and living on whatever kind of food people put into his bowl. He has made pilgrimages to sacred places and visited many wise old teachers and reputed saints. He wants to talk about God, about poverty and riches, about the soul and the body, about suffering and sin. Then he looks earnestly at you and says:

"Friend, I am searching for light on our human path. Nothing matters to me—I don't care where I eat or sleep—except my quest for spiritual truth. I am looking for God. Sometimes I hear him in a holy book; sometimes I see him in the dark pools of a mighty river; sometimes I smell him as the smoke drifts up from the fires in a little village. I am seeking not only with my mind but with my whole self which I open to whatever may come to me from him. I know nothing of the land you come from; but I have heard that, although you are very busy with the material things of this life, you also have holy men, you also have holy books, you also sometimes seek to know the Lord God and the world of spirit. One day in a hospital I met a woman from your country who was nursing the sick. She was very busy and didn't have much time to talk, but she said something about her religion, about the Jesus whom she worshiped. And I was told by others that she believed in the Christian gospel. Tell me, what is this Christian gospel?"

Well, there I leave you in our little fantasy, face to face with a deeply sincere and infinitely tolerant and receptive seeker after truth. What are you going to tell him? How do you begin to express what the Christian gospel has to say? Suppose you begin: "Well, we believe there is a God and we should love him with all our heart and mind and soul." He would certainly reply: "Yes, indeed, that is true. We must love him like that. But what is the Christian gospel?" You might add: "And we must love our neighbors as ourselves." And then he might say: "That indeed would be wonderful; many holy men have told us about this—but what is your Christian gospel?" Suppose you tried again and said: "The gospel says that if you're good you'll go to heaven." Then he would reply: "And if I'm not good then I suppose I'll go to hell. Is that your gospel, your good news because I'm not very good?"

Now, of course, I'm just guessing at some of the things you might say, and probably no two would come up with the same account of the gospel. But some of these attempts come close to what I've heard people say when struggling for a definition. And it's clear that even those who have been raised in a Christian tradition may still have a discovery to make as to what the gospel really is. There are lots of beliefs about God and about the good life which Christianity shares with other great religions. They are true; they are important, but they

77

are not the gospel. There would have been no need for a New Testament if the gospel were already revealed in the Old or in the other sacred writings that have inspired mankind. Surely every thoughtful person, whatever his convictions, must have some curiosity as to what this gospel is that the New Testament uniquely declares.

They were very curious in Galilee when Jesus suddenly appeared on the streets and the lakeside talking about the good news. They sensed something new, something exciting, something disturbing, and something strangely refreshing—but they didn't quite know what it was. They were equally curious in the towns and cities of the Roman Empire when, a little later, Paul arrived and spoke passionately about this gospel. You could say that the interest and curiosity died away when the Christian church got itself established in the succeeding centuries so that Christianity began to seem like the normal and accepted background of life, something to be taken for granted. But every now and then someone got curious about the gospel. Had it been smothered in the organization? Did people really know what it meant? And they delved back into the New Testament and were amazed at what they discovered. We are in such a period now. Older people may often think of the gospel as something they absorbed with the ABC's and the multiplication tables, but the younger generation are beginning to ask questions and to discover the gospel all over again as something amazingly new and exciting.

Well, what is it? Once again, words are a problem; for we're talking not about a theory but an experience, a power, an invasion of the spirit. That's why some discover the gospel through music, or drama, or painting, or—most likely of all—through the life of a parent or a friend. But the Bible says it in words—and word-pictures. So we ought to be able to in the vocabulary and imagery of today. Let me try.

The gospel has to do first and foremost with our relationship to God and, coincidentally, with our relationship to other people and to ourselves. And about all this it brings *liberating news.*

If anyone should ask: How can news be liberating? I sympathize with the difficulty, for most of the news we hear today has the opposite effect. The tale of wars and riots, crimes and graft, accidents and famines, is hardly liberating. Rather it seems to imprison us in a world where we begin to despair of ever finding room for hope and confidence in the future. But we still know something about the kind of news that sets us free. If you suspected that you were suffering from an inoperable cancer, and the medical examination revealed that nothing at all serious was the matter, that would be liberating news, wouldn't it? Just a few words from your doctor or a letter from the specialist, and you would feel as though the shackles had dropped off.

I once experienced liberating news that I shall never forget. In March, 1945, I was in a big stalag in the west of Germany. Most of us had been in one camp or another for five years, and—at last— the sound of the Allied guns began to be heard, and we knew that something was going to happen. Good Friday came and the entire camp was crouched within the huts waiting the outcome of a battle that seemed to be raging just outside the wire. At three o'clock in the afternoon I was conducting a service with an American unit and had spoken of the death of Jesus as the liberator of all mankind. We sang the Doxology, and then I heard a tremendous noise outside. The entire camp was pouring out of the huts and rushing to the gates. The word was "The Americans are here!" And—sure enough—roaring past the gates were the tanks and guns of General Patton's Third Army.

"The Americans are here!" That, for ten thousand of us, was liberating news. We were free. I have sometimes thought that I might have met some fellow prisoner at that moment moping on his bed. I could have given him the news, and he might have said: "Don't give me that stuff. I've heard these rumors before." He could have pointed out that we were still in the camp; the barbed wire and the sentry boxes were still there.

Theoretically, I suppose, he might just have stayed on—refusing to believe the liberating news.

The curious thing about the news concerning Jesus Christ and his liberating action is that a very great number refuse to believe it. They see nothing changed in the world fundamentally since he came. They hear a form of words about being reconciled to God, about being freed from our sins, about being re-created in Christ—but it sounds like old stuff with no meaning left in it. Yet it is still dynamite, this Christian gospel, even though it does sometimes seem too good to be true.

What is the essence of this liberating news? Surprisingly enough, it has nothing to do with rules and rituals or recipes for the religious life. It is a declaration that God, for Christ's sake, accepts us just as we are. While religious laws and ethical systems and church requirements all seem to tell us how to work our passage, how to justify ourselves in God's sight, the gospel simply tells us that Christ has done all this for us, has lived his perfect life for us, has died a sacrificial death for us, has returned in triumph from the grave for us, and we have nothing to do but accept his gift. In that stalag we were very conscious that we had not won our freedom. Other men had fought and died to reach us. All we could do was humbly and gratefully accept—and walk out as free men, free men with a sense of gratitude that should never leave us.

The whole New Testament throbs with this liberating news. Everything that Jesus did or said had to do with the freeing of men, women, and children from the bondage of their sins and releasing them from the pressure of guilt before God and man. He said that he had come "to seek and to save that which is lost," and he totally ignored the usual distinctions between "good people" and "bad people." In his eyes every one of us, no matter how moral or religious, is lost until we are found and redeemed by the love of God. No one can be too depraved, too enslaved by evil habit, to be reached by this love. Even in the hell of despair and utter loneliness this liberating power can reach us—for Jesus descended into that hell himself as he bled for our redemption. The only thing that can cut us off from this gospel of God's love and acceptance is the illusion that we don't really need it. The good news cannot be heard by those who think they are already good enough. That is why Jesus said, with reference to some religious people of his day, that "it is not the healthy that need a doctor, but the sick. . . . I did not come to invite virtuous people, but sinners." To this day it remains true that those who think they are virtuous cannot hear the liberating news. Paul saw into the heart of this gospel when he wrote that "Christ died for us while *we were yet sinners,* and that is God's own proof of his love toward us."

No one who has experienced in any way this

liberating news of God's love to us in Christ can possibly be arrogant or condescending to those of other faiths or of none at all. For we are merely the recipients of a grace we have not deserved, and in gratitude we try to share what we have received. Evangelism, which literally means passing on the liberating news, is not a matter of persuading someone else to accept *my* religion, but, as D. T. Niles of Ceylon used to say, it is simply one beggar telling another where to find bread. To the seeker after God we can give the news of God's seeking after us. To the moralist we confess that the only goodness we know is that which God confers on us in Christ. To the skeptic we tell the story of a Christ who works in this world and in our hearts with a transforming power.

Have you discovered this gospel? It's strange how often the familiar phrases and clichés of Christian evangelism get between us and the liberating news. We can listen to the texts of Scripture without really hearing the gospel, which Paul described once as "the saving power of God for everyone who has faith." A saving power—that's something different from a theory or even a philosophy of life. This saving power is what draws us into the communion with God as we realize that, in spite of all our sins, we are accepted by him. This saving power is what works in us to reconcile us with our fellowmen and to make us the instruments of God's peace. This saving power is the dynamic that lifts us beyond the grip of the passions that destroy us and the fears that paralyze us. This saving power is what liberates us from self hatred and despair. The one and only condition for receiving it is that we acknowledge our need and say yes to the liberating news. There are a thousand ways of saying yes, but in essence it means the conscious yielding of all that we know of ourselves to all that we have come to know of Christ.

8

Investigating Our Ancestors

Dr. George McLeod of Iona used to remark that many of the so-called Christian people of Scotland were really Confucians, and he went on to define a Confucian as "one who pays occasional visits to the shrines of his ancestors." That is not very fair to the great tradition of Confucianism, but I think you know what he was getting at. In this country, especially around Thanksgiving, Christmas, and Easter, there are a good many who pay these occasional visits to the shrines of their ancestors. Why? Have you ever been curious about this tug from the past which many seem to experience at certain times of the year? Men and women who get along from day to day without much thought about either God or their ancestors do apparently suffer from sudden spurts of conscience or twinges of nostalgia and find themselves in a church on Christmas Eve or saying an unaccustomed grace at the Thanksgiving dinner.

I want to investigate with you the meaning and the value of this pull from the past which is curiously associated with religious belief. Although I have often spoken about the dangers of identifying religion with the past and the absurdity of identifying God with the ancient and long ago, it remains true that Christianity is a historical religion and that all living faith has deep roots in past events. Therefore, it is natural that in a season when our thoughts go back to Pilgrims, the founding fathers, and to the ancestors who shaped the destiny of our country, we should stop to think about memory and tradition as factors in our social and religious life today. It's not just a sign of age to become concerned about our ancestors. We are never too young to do a little investigating of our heritage.

This is not a day when much attention is given to memories and stories from our past. We have been living through a period of intense national forgetfulness and are inclined to be impatient with anyone who wants us to spend time contemplating the past. It is understandable that a generation confronted with unique opportunities and dangers resulting from the breathtaking acceleration of scientific discovery should feel somewhat isolated from the world of the Pilgrims or of Lincoln or of

1917 or 1941. After all, though George Washington had his problems, he couldn't press a button to devastate half the globe. Grandmother, as we know, was very busy but lost no sleep worrying about nuclear weapons or heroin. For our ancestors the moon was a familiar companion, not a target. No previous generation has had to face a future of such unimaginable possibilities for good or evil. So it's no wonder many feel that we've parted company with past generations and see no point in keeping their memory alive. What have they to teach us? is the natural response.

So commemorations and ancestor investigation are not in style. The "now generation" turns away from historical ceremonies, from the remembrance of past heroes and "battles long ago," and even from the thought of grandfather's world, saying: "Let the dead bury their dead; we are concerned with justice *now*, with freedom *now*, with peace *now*." History seems a useless subject compared with psychology, sociology, or physics. Literature now means the modern novel, the poetry of today, the visions of tomorrow, science fiction; and the classics are left to gather dust. Religion, we are told *ad nauseam*, must be "relevant," by which is meant that the churches must be purged of their preoccupation with what happened two thousand years ago and solely concerned with the issue of the day. So away with the God of our fathers, let's find the God of our children; away with Isaiah and

87

Paul, let's hear from Marcuse and McLuhan; away, with the mumbo jumbo, let's celebrate man's coming of age.

There are now signs that we are emerging from this monstrous reign of the relevant, this overvaluing of the present moment. It was a natural response to the furious pace of recent events and to future shock. A reaction is setting in which is really a kind of recovery of nerve, a realization of our solidarity with our ancestors and of certain human qualities that we share with them. The emphasis is on humanity—the humanity we inherit from our ancestors which is endangered by some of the trends in our technological society. A whole new generation is discovering that the ancestral voices we hear in a musical like *Godspell,* a song like "Amazing Grace," or the novels of Hermann Hesse may be more important than the breathless comments of a reporter fresh from some new discovery of disaster.

It's not only the elderly who are feeling again the tug from the world of our ancestors. The young are indicating that they are getting tired of the everlasting Now and want to take at least an occasional trip to the strange and fascinating land of the past—even if they travel no farther than *No, No, Nanette.* The new romanticism is leading others to the Victorian era or the Middle Ages. It looks as though we are emerging from the period of frantic concern with today and finding again some sense of solidarity with our ancestors. However, in case some of us begin to feel smug about this rediscovery of the past and begin to talk like the author of the book of Ecclesiastes (whom I shall quote in a moment), we ought to remember that there is a right and a wrong way of being entranced with the days of old.

"The thing that hath been," says Ecclesiastes, "it is that which shall be; and that which is done is that which shall be done: and there is no new thing under the sun. Is there anything whereof it may be said, See, this is new? it hath already been of old time, which was before us." That's the voice of a somewhat cynical old man who believes that history repeats itself and likes to remind his juniors that "we've seen it all before." That's all very well as a warning against the tendency of each new generation to think that their problems, their ideals, their visions are unique; but it breeds a sterile conservatism—the kind of attitude that has consistently opposed every new idea, the good as well as the bad. There is a kind of ancestor worship that is mere nostalgia, the innocent conviction that things were really much better long ago.

The Latin poet Horace wrote long ago of the man he called *"Laudator temporis acti"*—the one who praises days gone by. This is how he describes him: "Testy, a grumbler, inclined to praise the way the world went when he was a boy, to play the critic and censor of the new generation." A

89

sense of history should not mean an idealizing of the past and a constant bewailing of the present. A real investigation of our ancestors and the world they lived in should free us from the legends on which such nostalgia feeds. We will learn, for instance, that this is not the first generation in America to experience crime, violence, and irreligion on a vast scale and that corruption in high places was sometimes much worse than it is today. We shall learn that there were periods in our history when the church was more bitterly divided than it is now, and had less hold on the loyalty of the population. The nostalgia of the old and the romanticism of the young are often no more than escapes from the tensions of today into some imagined utopia of the past.

Memory, personal and national, is a priceless asset—but there is a huge difference between this romantic nostalgia and the creative memory which is not only a refuge but a strength. The creative memory draws on the richest traditions of the past to inspire us to accept the challenges of today. It re-creates great events of history, not as a dream to divert our attention from the harsh realities we are now facing, but as a source of strength with which to meet them. It elicits from the past not wistful yearnings but living hope. When the author of the epistle to the Hebrews runs through the roll call of his nation's past heroes, he doesn't conclude by setting them on a pedestal and sighing that there are no such heroes left. Instead he goes on: "Wherefore seeing we also are compassed about with so great a cloud of witnesses, let us lay aside every weight, and the sin which doth so easily beset us, and let us run with patience the race that is set before us, looking unto Jesus the author and finisher of our faith."

This is the creative memory that the Bible sets before us. The entire book is, in fact, dominated by the thought of two great ancestral events which are kept mysteriously alive in the memory of God's people.

In the Old Testament one dominating theme sounds in nearly every book—the memory of the Exodus of Israel from Egypt. Now there was a temptation to hark back to those great days of the famous liberation in the wrong spirit. There were those who were apt to say: "Those were the days—when Moses was alive and when God was clearly seen to be active in human affairs," just as there is in every church today the old member who keeps recalling the great days when everything was so wonderful, so spiritual, and so enthusiastic. But time and again the Israelites were told that the purpose of remembering was not to long for the past but to grasp the future. The word of the Lord to Joshua was: "As I was with Moses, so I will be with thee: I will not fail thee, nor forsake thee. Be strong and of good courage." That is creative memory. The prophets, who were continually re-

91

minding the people of the days when God brought their ancestors up out of Egypt, were the very men who insisted on their meeting the challenges of the new day. The Exodus for them was not a distant event to be commemorated once a year with nostalgic rites, but a living sign of God's purpose for his people, a stimulus for the nation's faith in a day of decadence. This is why they urged the people to "look unto the rock whence ye are hewn, and to the hole of the pit whence ye are digged."

The second great event to which the people of God look back today is, for Christians, the resurrection of Jesus Christ. Just as Israel finds constant, living inspiration in the remembrance of the Exodus, so Christians keep in mind the cosmic liberation that came with the life, death, and resurrection of Jesus. In thousands of churches today there is a table on which are written these words: "This do in remembrance of me." What happens when Christians gather round that table is not nostalgia, a sentimental recollection that a certain Jesus once died on a cross and now lives in a happy land, far, far away. The word "remember" here means the re-creation of this tremendous event as a living power and a communion with this Jesus as a living Lord. Creative memory of this kind is not a yearning but a refreshment. And its note is not gloom but joy.

So when we begin to think again about our ancestors in this land and about that greater heritage that sweeps backward to the apostles and prophets, we can make the discovery that there is a strength on which we can draw, a renovating power in the living past. Without this creative memory an individual or a nation is fatally weakened and becomes a prey to the forces of tyranny, anarchy, and destruction. Totalitarianism in all its forms has always been confronted by the courageous resistance of the men and women of creative memory. The true revolutionary is the man who fights for freedom in the strength of a living and sacred tradition. George Washington was such a man. So was Abraham Lincoln. So was Winston Churchill. And those who have been the most effective leaders of the black struggle for freedom in our time have drawn their strength from the creative memory of a living religion: "Let my people go."

If, then, this message should evoke in you a new curiosity about these ancestors of ours, a new desire to discover the basic faith that sustained the greatest of them in times of equal danger and opportunity to our own, then a visit to the "shrine of our ancestors" will have been worthwhile. It is not an escape to a temple of nostalgia where we sit and sigh for the "good old days." It is a movement of thanksgiving whereby we are humble enough to remember what we owe and to acknowledge that we are not left to our own frail resources as we face the future. It is a search for that strength of a thankful heart which alone can direct today's revolution to positive and creative ends. It is the expression of our desire to accept with joy the challenge of change so that the God of our fathers may still be the God of our children.

9

The Most Curious Book in the World

When I was in the Army there were two nick-names for a chaplain that are probably now completely out of date. One was "God-botherer," which was used with affectionate irony, suggesting that the chaplain was the man whose job it was to keep pestering God with prayers and services. The other was "Bible-puncher"—and the reference is obvious.

Now I don't mind being called a "God-botherer" if it implies that God is someone with whom I talk regularly, and I have pretty good authority for believing that he likes being "bothered" in this way. Jesus said once that his disciples "should keep on praying and never lose heart," and he illustrated the point by a very unexpected story about a widow who kept pestering a judge to give a verdict in her favor. You've probably heard the remark: "He doesn't bother the church much." Well, in that sense I'd rather earn the name "God-botherer" than have in my obituary that "he didn't bother God much."

As for "Bible-puncher"—if we forget for a moment the image of some wild-eyed preacher thumping the Book and consigning his hearers to hell—I don't mind the name at all. In fact, I'd rather people felt that my sermons were punched out of the Bible than derived from any other source. The longer I'm at the job of preaching, the more dependent I am on the content of the Bible. The more tense and difficult the world in which we live, the more need I feel for something more than the contents of my own mind or the wisdom of my contemporaries.

Now that's curious, isn't it? You would think that after thirty-five years of preaching from the Bible (which is where I am now) one would be nearly finished with it and desperately searching for other sources of inspiration. And it might be expected that the more our modern world develops problems and possibilities unheard of two thousand years ago, the less the Bible might have something helpful to say. Yet I am finding the opposite to be true. Nearly every week I discover insights and illuminations in the Bible that I had previously missed which have a great deal to say to the questions that are agitating us now.

That's very strange when you consider that the books of the Bible were written by men who lived in a totally different culture from ours and were completely ignorant of the science and technology that have shaped the modern world. It's even more strange when you realize that they were all, with one exception, members of one tiny group among all the nations—the Jewish people—and that the entire collection of books is soaked in their way of life, their history, and their particular problems. If the odds are against any packet of ancient literature speaking effectively to the late twentieth century, they are even greater when such books are the product of one tiny community that was continually being swallowed up in the conflicts of the major powers.

What is it that gives this book its incredible staying power? Admittedly there are literary classics which survive the centuries—Homer, Vergil, Plato, Dante, Shakespeare, to name a few—but who ever heard of a worldwide organization of hundreds of millions devoted to reading publicly from their works today? Or which of them ever burst on the modern world in a paperback that breaks all records like the recent *Good News for Modern Man?* Can any of them equal the Bible in universal appeal? The Bible is, after all, from the literary point of view an astonishing assortment of history, poetry, drama, legend, aphorism, epistle, apocalyptic, and oratory of unequal value, almost carelessly cited and translated from Hebrew and first-century vernacular Greek. Yet this is the book that has made, and still makes, such an impact on ordinary people in every land that it changes lives, nourishes hope, creates faith, and penetrates to every level of national life. You might believe it impossible for any thinking man or woman to avoid being curious about this unique phenomenon in the world of books.

But many do. They succeed in acquiring an education in which the Bible only enters indirectly. They know of its existence, but they never bother really to examine its contents. In spite of the huge sales comparatively few in our generation are really familiar with the Bible. Ask the average person where the phrase "God tempers the wind to the shorn lamb" comes from, and he will say "the Bible"—but it doesn't. If you told him it came from the book of Hezekiah he'd probably believe you— but there is no such book. A student coming out of chapel one day was heard to remark: "That's funny about Dan and Beersheba—I always thought they were man and wife, like Sodom and Gomorrah." If you don't think that's funny, then you're not really familiar with the Bible. But these are mere straws in the wind. More important is the sad fact that thousands of educated, sensible people don't take the trouble to find out what this book contains in any systematic way. Perhaps their curiosity is dulled by the repellant appearance of the old style

Bible with its black covers and tiny print. Or, more likely, they have written off the Bible as a religious book—and they claim not to be concerned about religion at all.

In this sense it's often sheer prejudice that keeps a man or woman from being interested in the Bible—I mean prejudice in its literal sense of forming a judgment before examining the fact. People make the prejudgment that the Bible is a dull, religious book with nothing to say to bright, irreligious people. If they had the curiosity to start reading it in some palatable edition, they might discover that it is neither dull nor is it, strictly speaking, religious.

Admittedly, there are portions of it which anyone might find wearisome if he plunged in without preparation, but taken as a whole, the Bible contains not only some of the most exciting reading anywhere but a stupendous, mind-blowing conception of the meaning of human life and the ultimate destiny of mankind. And when I say that it is not, strictly speaking, a religious book, I mean that it contains very little of the kind of material you find in the literature that goes under the title of religion in your local bookstore. It has very little to say about theology, if by that we mean the attempt to expound systematically doctrines about God and man. It has no treatises on prayer or the world to come. There is not too much about organized worship—practically nothing in the New

Testament. It contrasts strongly with classical religious books, both Christian and non-Christian. It is much more concrete, much more earthy, much less abstract, much less philosophical.

Here is one of the strange paradoxes of the Bible. No other book has ever brought ordinary people into such living contact with God; yet it contains very little instruction about what we call the religious life, contains much that we would today consider of purely secular interest, and has one book that doesn't even mention God at all. If this rouses our curiosity we shall find out that the reason for this apparent paradox is that the Bible doesn't recognize religion as a special department of life with its own regulations and ways of thought. It proclaims a God who is concerned with the whole of life, with the material as well as the spiritual. "The earth is the Lord's and the fulness thereof" we read in one of the psalms, and that means for biblical writers that God is active everywhere and all the time. He cannot be escaped any more than he can be defined. The Bible writers are not concerned with abstract definitions of God's being, but with his universal action.

There is a curious, indirect way in which we encounter God in the Bible. That is, we don't learn to say "God is thus and thus," but we come to know him in action, in his reflection in nature and the world of men. Some years ago I copied this from a book called *The Bible View of Life,* by S. C. Carpenter: "It was observed long ago that, when the moon shines, we say: 'The moon is beautiful.' When the sun shines, we say: 'How beautiful earth is.' That is the Bible view of life." In other words, in the Bible we don't find ourselves staring, as it were, into the face of God. We find his reflection, and we find it everywhere.

This is the explanation of the other paradox—that the book which brings us into the divine dimension, the book that has expanded the mind and soul of millions, the book that brings us into the presence of God and stings us with the sense of our unholiness, the book that overwhelms us with the news of his amazing grace, is a book written by men with their eyes generally fixed on the practical things of this material world, by men of limited experience and often narrowly national outlook, by men of whom only a few could be considered brilliant thinkers or outstandingly cultured writers. It is through the words of real men, people like us describing the joys and sorrows, hopes and fears, daily adventures, and social and political problems of a truly human community, that we find the word of God coming through.

What do I mean by the word of God? Well, words are the curious sounds or forms by which we communicate. We communicate our thoughts —as I am trying to do now to you. But words do more. They communicate something of ourselves. You are not only receiving (I am bold to hope) some of my thoughts; you are, at least in part, receiving *me*. In a literal sense every time I open my mouth I give myself away. When we read the Bible expectantly—not just as a literary collection but looking for something that might change our lives—we find ourselves being mysteriously addressed by the living God. In other words, the one responsible for all that exists is disclosing himself to us. It's not just information about himself he discloses. It is himself. And the climax of this disclosure comes with the Gospels where we read that "The Word was made flesh and dwelt among us . . . full of grace and truth." The Bible culminates in the revelation of Jesus Christ in whom God simply gives himself to us. What all else in the Bible has prepared us for—the revelation of God through human words and actions—is climaxed now in the story of the one true man who is also truly God.

Perhaps someone may feel like saying: "Now you've lost me." Perhaps I have, but if you stay around with the Bible, you will find that God has not lost you. He's looking for you there. We don't all meet him in the same way. He hasn't the same thing to say to each of us. The Bible has an extraordinary way of reaching all kinds of people— young and old, Eastern and Western, powerful and weak, brilliant and dull. It has spoken to individuals through one single verse and turned them upside down; it has spoken to others through the total impact of a book or the whole Book; it has changed the moral climate of nations; it has been a revolutionary force in times of tyranny; it has been a stabilizer in times of confusion; it has been a re-creative power in times of decadence. And all this happens because this curious book is at the same time truly human and truly divine.

That is what the inquirer finds most difficult to understand. He wants either a purely human collection of literature which he can read with enjoyment without being troubled about either his way of life or the destiny of the world. Or else he wants a purely divine book which will tell him exactly who God is and what his religious duties are. The Bible is neither. Some have robbed it of its power by claiming that it is no different from any other collection of ancient literature and should be regarded more or less as a museum piece to be analyzed by the historian and the literary critic. Others equally rob it of its power by some theory whereby its writers cease to be really human and were mere microphones for an infallible recording by the Spirit of God. To ignore the true humanity of the Bible is to misunderstand it and to draw some dangerous conclusions. To ignore the true divinity of it is to miss the chance of being grasped and saved by the living God and experiencing life in a new dimension.

The poet Coleridge once said that the reason

why he was convinced of the inspiration of the Bible was not that he was persuaded by all kinds of arguments for its divine origin, but simply, he said, "because this Book finds me." Will you give it another chance?

10

Just What Can I Do?

A rhetorical question, we used to be told in our grammer class, is one that neither expects nor needs an answer. When a politician in an election campaign asks: "Who is more qualified than Mr. X to represent us in Congress?" he doesn't expect you to come up with a list of names. When a cheerful friend says: "What's the use of worrying?" you're not supposed to tell him. When a crowd of kids chant: "Two, four, six, eight; who do we appreciate?" they assume you know the answer.

One rhetorical question that is spoken or muttered by thousands today is: "What can *I* do?" We seem to be living at a time when people are more worried than usual about all kinds of things they feel are wrong and at the same time feel unusually helpless. The reason why we are exceptionally worried is partly that more worry material is fed to us than to any previous generation. Not a crime or a massacre or a disaster or an outbreak of hostilities can happen anywhere in the world without it being brought to our attention almost at once. The sheer load of trouble that is dumped on us daily is enough to paralyze even the most sensitive, and we sit in front of our television sets or radios feeling utterly powerless to help. What can *I* do?—a purely rhetorical question, expecting no answer but a shrug of the shoulders.

Yet every now and then I hear these words in an entirely different tone of voice. A new member in a big city church, for instance, gets caught up in the excitement of the program and wants very much to be part of it. "What can *I* do?" he or she asks the pastor, and wants a definite answer. Or perhaps someone gets fired up by a campaign for some social or political cause and shows up immediately at the volunteer desk asking: "What can *I* do? Give me a job." Or it may be that you or I wake up one day to a new range of activities, all kinds of things that we never attempted before—writing, painting, growing things, running a youth club, visiting the sick, acting, modeling, exploring a new area, preserving the countryside—and we suddenly say, What can *I* do? I never thought of that before."

The difference between merely existing and really living can be measured by these two ways of saying the same thing. If we get into the habit of using the rhetorical question: "What can *I* do?"

we gradually contract out of life and resign ourselves to sitting on the sidelines waiting for things
to happen. If, on the other hand, we are aroused to
ask the real question: "What can *I* do?" with some
lively expectation of finding the answer, then we
really begin to live. Have you ever thought that
part of what the New Testament means by conver-
sion is this turning from the passive, hopeless,
shoulder-shrugging attitude to the active, hopeful,
and tenaciously believing? I have been speaking in
this book of curiosity as a gateway to living religion, and I truly believe that when we become
curious enough to raise the genuine question:
"What can *I* do?" a door opens to a new life in
which God and our neighbor are no longer dim
abstractions but exciting realities. It was surely this
that was indicated by the words of Jesus: "I am
come that they might have life and that they might
have it more abundantly." This is the spirit in
which he came to earth—"What can *I* do? I must
be about my Father's business." Can you imagine
him, faced as he was with such appalling obstacles
as the might of imperial Rome, the hostility of the
religious establishment, and the apathy of the
majority of the population, sitting down and saying in that other tone of voice: "What can *I* do?"
He chose life—and he chose it for us all.

Ever since we have had a child around in our
home, I keep finding new meaning in what Jesus
said about becoming "as little children," as the

107

secret of this new life he came to bring. One of these meanings is right here. Does a little child ever give the impression of utter boredom and hopelessness? As he grows up in these early years do we hear him saying with a sigh of resignation: "What can *I* do?" Don't we rather watch him reaching out in boundless curiosity and expectation into constantly new horizons of joyful activity? "What can *I* do? What can *I* do next?" Jesus indicated that real living, life in his kingdom, means turning around, converting, so that we abandon the old attitudes of helpless resignation and reach out again like a child to the infinite possibilities of satisfying activity.

I hope that nobody thinks that I am contrasting a quiet, gentle, philosophical frame of mind with a frenetic activism and pleading for everyone to get busy, no matter how, in the name of religion. That's not the point at all. I remember how in that home in Bethany, Jesus appreciated the quiet, undemonstrative Mary sitting listening at his feet and gently rebuked that fussy activist, her sister, Martha, who, the Bible says, "was cumbered about with much serving." I think we all know people in our day who are "cumbered about with much serving." Martha wanted to hear Mary saying "What can *I* do?" but, in fact, she had answered the question—and Jesus said she had chosen well. The choice is not between the quiet, meditative life and the rushing around; it is between cynical apathy and coming alive.

It is always a danger signal for a nation when too many people begin to feel helpless and insignificant, as though they could have no influence whatever on the course of events. When more and more begin to say, "What can *I* do?" as if the will and the action of an individual is powerless against the anonymous forces that rule us, then real democracy begins to die, and we are on the way to another form of government. Every tyrant from the days of the Greeks to Hitler and Stalin has been given his opportunity by a majority of people who had ceased to believe in their own capacity to influence the shape of events. Our liberties and opportunities depend much more than we realize on our conviction that our voice does count in determing the way the nation goes. When we cease to believe this, when we resign any hope of effecting changes or influencing policies, we prepare the way for the demagogue and the dictator. Such abdication leads also to the mood of frustration and bitterness that corrupts, degrades, and divides a nation. For when men and women give up hope of influencing a society for good, they are apt to concentrate their energies on destructive criticism and petulant complaint. If we find ourselves increasingly inclined to deplore and bewail, to judge and condemn, then we may suspect that

109

we are victims of the paralysis of apathy: "Just what can I do?"

It's easy to understand why this paralysis is striking so many today. We live in an age of unparalleled bigness—big government, big business, big organizations, big social and ecclesiastical structures. In spite of the constant talk abut participation the average citizen finds it hard to believe that he participates in any real sense in the decisions of government—federal, state, or local; in the running of the organization that employs him; in the control of the mass media that supply him with news and entertainment; in the determining of priorities of value in society; or even in the pronouncements and activities of the religious denomination he belongs to. But it's not only the bigness that robs him of a sense of responsibility—it's the anonymity. Increasingly people are feeling that the shots are being called by faceless groups who wield great power but are not apparently accountable to anyone. "They" are going to change our environment; "they" are polluting the atmosphere; "they" are going to program the future, to decide what kind of babies shall be born, to control human destiny. But nobody knows just who "they" are. If "they" are really in charge, just what can *I* do?"

This is where a little healthy curiosity comes in. We might start asking: "Has it been true in the past that the ordinary man and woman has counted for nothing? Sure, they have been continually at the mercy of powers and forces beyond their control, but is it not true that at great moments in human history the voice of the individual has been heard, and the destiny of nations decided by a multitude of ordinary men and women with conviction and resolution?" Would Paul and the other apostles have turned the world upside down without the devotion and prayers and actions of thousands of whom only a few names have been left in corners of the New Testament? Did Luther and Calvin set about to reform the church on their own, or was the entire movement not dependent on the beliefs and actions of people like you and me whose names are completely forgotten? Was 1776 the work of a few leaders who signed the Declaration of Independence, or was it the upsurge of thousands of ordinary people who never stopped to ask: "Just what can *I* do," but went ahead and did it? Was it Winston Churchill on his own who defied the Nazis in 1940, or was he, as he himself put it, "the lion's roar"—the lion being the wills of millions of determined individuals? It's good for us to ferret around a little in history when we are tempted to think that the individual counts for nothing in the destiny of nations.

Just as the man or woman of faith is not going to be bullied by sheer bigness, so we are going to stand up against another debilitating influence in the climate of our times. I refer to the constant suggestion that we are not really responsible beings able to choose our course and throw our weight behind the causes in which we believe. A stream of books and articles have appeared in recent years tending to reduce the stature of mankind to the level of the animal or vegetable world. Some emphasize our kinship with the beasts and see our current problems in the light of the instinctual behavior of the birds, the bees, or the monkeys. Others claim that we are entirely at the mercy of our genes and have no more freedom of choice than a twig blowing in the wind. One way or another, the status of the individual as a person of dignity and potential is undermined, and humanity becomes just so much more material to be manipulated and controlled.

Fortunately no one as yet really acts as if this analysis were true. Even the propounders of these theories must believe in the possibility of free persuasion—otherwise they wouldn't bother writing books to convince us. And we have not yet arrived at the point where we stop using the words "good" and "bad," "right" and "wrong." The moment we make a judgment of value we assume that men and women are uniquely responsible beings. And we have the right to ask those who claim that human beings are so much material to be controlled just who is going to do the controlling. If science gives us the possibility of deciding what kind of men and women are to be born in the future, won't someone have to decide that one kind of human being is better than another? And isn't that a free and, let us hope, responsible decision?

If we do sometimes sadly realize the limits of our powers as free creatures, there is no need to despair and cry: "Just what can *I* do?" The Bible already indicates to us the limiting factors on our freedom of choice and sets man's ability to choose and to control within the sovereign pattern of the will of God. Yet that same Bible on nearly every page insists on the responsibility of men and women to choose what is good and so to determine the moral climate of a society or nation. "Choose ye this day whom ye will serve" is the word of the Old Testament, and in the New we meet Jesus—a Jesus whom we cannot imagine as the mere product of his environment, a puppet in the hands of the blind forces of nature. He is the one whom his followers see as the Son of God, saying to his Father: "What can *I* do?" and choosing the way of obedience right to the cross. And he is the one who said of individual human beings, "You are of value."

Therefore, all who are discovering this timeless message of the Bible ought to rejoice today in every sign that ordinary people are refusing to be the victims of anonymous powers and are demanding to be heard as men and women of freedom and dignity, made in the image of the Father God. And our weight should be thrown behind all that exalts true humanity and fortifies the conviction that, after all, there *is* something I can do. For the Christian, baffled by the complexities of our age and sometimes despairing of the effect of our prayers or our feeble efforts to serve, this is the time to hear again the words: "I can do all things through Christ who strengthens me."

11

Where Did Jesus Come From?

Anyone who has traveled abroad is familiar with a formality connected with registering at a hotel. You are presented with a little slip to fill out giving information about yourself and your journey. One line reads: "Coming from . . . going to. . . ." I understand this goes to the local police so that you can be traced if somebody wants to find you in an emergency; so I suppose it is important to fill it out. But a friend of mine who is allergic to forms of any kind once told me that he consistently wrote "Coming from . . . *home*" and "Going to . . . *heaven*"—and so far no one had questioned these statements.

"Where do you come from?" The question normally means: "What's your hometown?" It's one of the commonest questions when we get talking with a stranger on a plane or at a party or a coffee hour after church. It's part of our natural curiosity about one another. Perhaps we have already tried to guess from the accent or the appearance, or else we are looking for a point of contact—"Then you must know such-and-such or so-and-so." It helps to identify a stranger when we know where he comes from.

Some parents believe in teaching a child a very precise answer to this question at an early age so that if he should ever get lost he can say "44 Chestnut Avenue, Squaresville," and be sent right home. But those same parents are later going to be confronted with the very same question in a different context. "Where do I come from?" asks the four-year-old and will not be satisfied with his home address. This is the point where the parent has to find another answer—unless he is like the father immortalized in the phrase: " 'Shut up!' he explained." Roughly speaking, the answer will be either scientific or religious—or, at best, a combination of the two. In other words, the parent will say: "From inside your mother," or "From God."

On the scientific level I believe a child has a right to be told the truth and not given fairy tales about storks or gooseberry bushes. Why should we hide from children their origin in the womb? The next question, however, goes beyond the physical facts. Have we an equal duty to indicate another dimension to the story of our origin by saying that we come from God? The answer to this will depend, of course, on the religious convictions of the parent. Many of us would have no hesitation in conveying, as we best can, the thought that ultimately our life springs from the mind and will of the Creator, the heart of our God. I believe that to be equally true with the scientific statement. Physically, we come from our mother's womb. But the mystery of the self, the unique individual, the soul, can be traced back only to the Creative Spirit who makes us, as the Bible says, "in his image."

I would suggest that even those who are too uncertain about their beliefs to speak to a child about God will want to convey something of the mystery surrounding the appearance on earth of a new life with all its potential for good or evil, a life that has never been and will never be duplicated in the story of the universe. To confine ourselves to the physical facts is to rob human life of its deepest meaning. Therefore, an agnostic parent need not feel hypocritical in exposing a child to the answers of religion. Whatever his own hesitations about the traditional language of religion, he must want his child to sense something of the mystery it enshrines. "Where do I come from?" and "Where am I going?" are questions that haunt every intelligent and naturally curious man or woman.

The specific question, however, that I am trying to answer now is: "Where did *Jesus* come from?"

117

It's a question that is natural at the time of the year when across the world millions are preparing to celebrate his birth. Unless we just accept Christmas as a folk festival to be enjoyed without any reflection about the meaning of the birth of Jesus, we are bound to have some curiosity about this celebration. No other religion makes such a fuss about the birth of its founder. Why have Christians felt that there was something unique about this event? What is the meaning of the stories that are told about angels and shepherds and wise men? Why these pictures of Mary and her Son with the light of heaven around them? Why the mystery about this conception? The alert and curious spirit will find many paths to explore among the narratives and poems that cluster around the birth of Jesus.

Where did he come from? As with anyone else we can give the physical answer: from his mother. Few people today would find anything worth special notice in that blunt statement of fact. But it was not always so. There was a time when some believers were so dazzled by the glory of a Christ whom they worshiped as Lord and Savior that they found it impossible to accept that his actual birth was the same as that of anyone else. They felt he must have appeared from heaven in some divine flash, without father or mother, and could not have gone through the normal processes of human birth. Even today there are Christians who

118

have never fully accepted in their mind or imagination this real humanity of Jesus. That is why they set down in the creed the word "born," which otherwise seems a superfluous statement. He was born of Mary: that is the first answer.

But we can, of course, go on to say that he came from the Jewish people, that he came from the region of Galilee at a certain point in history. That's another part of the answer and has its own importance. That Jesus was a Jew who lived when his country was occupied by the Romans explains a good deal about him—his language, his imagery, his style of life, his religious background, his mode of living, his sense of humor. Before we start making any claims about his universality as Son of Man, we have to reckon with his Jewishness. "Son of man" is itself an intensely Hebrew expression. All modern research on this section of history confirms the authenticity of the Gospel picture of the people and the land to which he belonged. Anyone who is genuinely curious about the origins of Jesus would have to start with this particular place and people—and, therefore, would soon have to begin studying again the book we call the Old Testament. You must have noticed how, for instance, the opening chapters of Luke's Gospel are steeped in the language and atmosphere of the prophets and the psalmists.

So this is where Jesus came from—from this people who, in the course of an extraordinary history of success and failure, religious fervor and apostasy, freedom and oppression and constant threat of annihilation, had produced a succession of unique spokesmen for God and man. So Jesus might well be located there. He came from out of this tumultuous history, and we can understand him as one of these prophets. For millions today, including many Jews, this is the explanation of Jesus. There is no difficulty in finding parallels in the writings of his people to a great many of his sayings, and he was not the first prophet to be suddenly silenced by a cruel death.

Why then should we pursue the question further? This is where he came from, and there is enough to account for much of the impact he has made upon the world. This is also where Moses came from, and Amos, and Isaiah. Yes, but suppose we raise the religious question concerning him and start asking in what sense he came from God. We begin to come across some startling claims. The birth narratives in Matthew and Luke speak of a unique relationship between this child and God. There is the voice that Mary heard saying: "The Holy Spirit will come upon you, and the power of the Most High will overshadow you; therefore the child to be born will be called holy, the Son of God." (Luke 1:35 RSV.) And there is the mysterious saying: "He shall be called Emmanuel, a name which means 'God is with us.' " The Fourth Gospel reaches even further into the

120

mystery and begins with the thought of the eternal word, or revelation, of God. "In the beginning was the Word, and the Word was with God, and the Word was God." Then, a little later, comes the astonishing statement: "And the Word was made flesh, and dwelt among us, and we beheld his glory."

Here we are in the presence of answers to our question that baffle the mind and stagger the imagination. We are being told that ultimately the origin of Jesus is nothing other than the life of God himself. While all of us owe our being to the will of the Creator, he is said to have existed in the heart and mind of God from all eternity. We are now beyond what can be adequately put into words, but it is a striking fact that those who saw him and lived with him came to tell in the end that nothing less than this could be said about him. He is the expression of God himself in human form. Therefore, in a unique way he came to our world from the eternal world of the divine.

Once when I was sitting in a student club in a university town, a bearded young man who was having tea with a couple of girls suddenly sprang to his feet and said loudly enough for all to hear: "I didn't ask to be born into this world," and went crashing out through the door. I was left pondering. "I didn't ask to be born into this world." True enough: neither did I. I doubt, however, whether—no matter how disgruntled he

121

was with life—he was really regretting his existence. It's strange how practically none of us would really like to have passed up the chance of existence, no matter how roughly life may have treated us. We'd rather be than not be—as Hamlet finally decided. Yet we certainly didn't ask to be born. But my thoughts went further that day. There was one person who really did ask to be born—and that was Jesus.

It may be that someone is wondering whether these thoughts about the origin of Jesus were not developed long after he had died, if the church had not projected on to a simple prophet some strange theological theories from other sources. Paul usually gets blamed for this, although there is a surprising unanimity among all the New Testament writers in making the unique claim for Jesus. Well, why don't we examine some of the things he said himself about his origin? The Fourth Gospel is, of course, full of amazing statements of this kind. "I and my Father are one." "Before Abraham was, I am." But some would say that this book has been colored by these later ideas and cannot be taken as direct evidence for the actual words of Jesus. Without arguing that point, we can turn to Mark's Gospel, which I once heard a skeptic describe as the one "that didn't seem to have been messed around with by someone who wanted to prove something."

I find there, right at the beginning, the story of Jesus' baptism in the river Jordan where it is recorded that a voice "came from heaven, Thou art my beloved Son; with thee I am well pleased" (Mark 1:11 RSV). That sounds as though Jesus was conscious of what we would call a special relationship to God, at least from this point on. Right through the Gospel we find him speaking and acting as though his origin was unique. He claimed to forgive sins, and this was always regarded as the divine prerogative. He acted as though a new event had taken place with his coming: "The time has come: the kingdom of God is upon you." Then there is the remarkable saying about the purpose of his life: "Even the Son of Man did not come to be served but to serve, and to give his life as a ransom for many."

That saying alone, from Mark's Gospel, could open wide horizons from the curious inquirer about where Jesus came from, and why he came. Let me in conclusion simply fasten on the expression he uses, not only here but constantly in the Gospels. "I am come." "The Son of Man has come." You and I don't ever think of describing our lifework in such terms. We might go so far as to say: "I believe I was born to be a doctor, or a minister, or a singer, or an artist," but we would not say "I have come. . . ." Yet Jesus consistently used this phrase. He is the one who came—came

123

from the inner world of spirit, the very real world of God; came from the heart of God himself. And he came to bring each one of us back to the home of the Father. That is why we sing: "Joy to the world! the Lord is come!"

12

Bethlehem - Let's Keep the Mystery

"Never complain; never explain"—that was the advice the wily old statesman Benjamin Disraeli used to give to his juniors, and I have been thinking that there is some wisdom here for those of us who preach the Christian gospel.

"Never complain"—that should go without saying. I've just been re-reading Paul's letter to the Philippians, which he wrote when in a prison cell, and there's not a breath of complaint in it. In fact, it's one of the most joyful books in the Bible. Yet somehow we do hear a note of complaint from the churches today, and sermons sometimes sound as if the preacher was thoroughly disgruntled with everything and everybody in the modern world. And who is going to be interested in good news given with a grudge? "Never complain" is good biblical advice for every Christian. It's the obverse of the apostolic injunction: "In everything give thanks." After all, it is Thanksgiving that we celebrate, not grumble-giving.

But how about: "Never explain"? Surely, you might say, that's precisely my job—to explain the meaning of the gospel, the contents of the Bible and how they relate to our life in America today. Every Sunday people come to church expecting to have some aspect of belief or Christian living explained to them. And doesn't every parent have to explain his religious convictions to his children? Since the gospel, with all that it says about God and Christ and the purpose of life, is by no means obviously true and acceptable for millions in our world, don't we owe them an explanation as to why we believe it?

As one who has spent a good deal of his life trying to explain these things, I have to admit the force of these objections. Yet the words "never explain" continue to haunt me. Disraeli never offered any explanation of his convictions and actions. He was simply warning against our habit of trying to justify everything we do or say. Our three-year-old agrees with him exactly; for whenever we ask him: "Now why did you do that, Rory?" he inevitably replies: "Because I did."

I know that we are living in a time when few are willing to accept what we call dogmatic religion. So we hear a great deal about dialogue, and feedback, and open forums. That's all to the good, for it means that people are not content with secondhand faith, believing simply on the say-so of some preacher or church. If you were to ask me why you should believe that God was in Christ reconciling the world to himself, I wouldn't answer: "Because I say so." I should be more likely to answer as Jesus did to the curious in his day: "Come and see." And I hope that I would be ready to listen to all the objections and difficulties that might be raised. But there does come a point in this matter of faith, you know, when explanations cease. And when someone says: "How can you go on believing in the love of God in a world like ours?" the ultimate answer must sound very like: "Because I do." There is a mystery of ultimate commitment that cannot be rationalized.

At the very deepest level of our experience we are always out of the reach of explanations. You don't explain just how you are moved almost to tears by a great performance of Shakespeare or Beethoven. A true artist doesn't explain his pictures. How do you explain your admiration for a soldier who flings himself on a live grenade to save the lives of his comrades or your sense of the sublime when the sun goes down in glory behind the mountains? And what about the overwhelming experiences of human love? Did Robert Burns explain anything when he wrote:

127

O my luve's like a red, red rose
That's newly sprung in June;
O my luve's like the melodie
That's sweetly played in tune.

I am reminded of John Donne's outburst: "For God's sake hold your tongue, and let me love."

So this is why I am saying about Bethlehem, about the Christmas story, let's keep the mystery. If we really believe in the churches that something unique happened when Jesus was born, that this really was the personal coming of Almighty God into our human life, that this was the beginning of a world-transforming drama culminating in a cruel death and a real resurrection, then, of course, there must be mystery, a feeling of awe and wonder, a sense of events beyond the grasp of any human mind, of a glory no one wants to analyze. I don't want anyone poking in to explain just who the angels were, or working out astronomically what star or comet might have been moving across the sky that particular year, or clarifying for me the question of the census, or the stable, or the wise men from the East. I don't want someone to make the Incarnation sound like the simplest and most natural thing in the world. In other words, I wouldn't smash the windows of Chartres Cathedral so that the light could shine in and we might see better.

In all this I believe the instincts of the ordinary person—even the non-Christian—have been sounder than those of many recent theologians and interpreters of the faith. For the tendency has been to reduce the Christian gospel to something so innocuous that no real leap of faith is required to believe it. Anything miraculous, or supernatural, has been explained away, and it has been assumed that the religiously curious are on the hunt for a set of beliefs that fit neatly into our secular world. Meanwhile, thousands of the genuinely curious have been bypassing this floodlit version of the gospel to seek truth in the shadows beyond the churches—ranging from the great mystics of the East to the local astrologer. It has at last been discovered that the so-called modern mind is not, after all, insensitive to mystery and revolted by the supernatural. On the contrary, there has not been for generations so much rummaging in the occult, so much yearning for the transcendent, so much hunger for a God who "moves in a mysterious way his wonders to perform." The "relevant religion" about which there was so much talk has turned out to be relevant only to minds incapable of stretching beyond the physical facts, and spirits devoid of imagination. So my plea is, let's keep and let's glory in the mystery.

This does not mean that we must silence the questions of the mind about the data of the New Testament. Still less does it mean that it doesn't matter whether or not these things really happened. There is a difference between mystery and mystification, or mumbo jumbo. The Christian gospel is squarely based on historical fact. Jesus did "come in the flesh," as the apostles put it, and I am not proposing that we neglect the solid, everyday realities recounted in the Gospels. I am not saying that the miracles are more important than the Sermon on the Mount. It is simply a question of recognizing that the impact of the story of Jesus brings us ultimately to the supreme mystery of his Person—when we have to take a leap of faith. Mystery stands at the frontier between the physical facts of this world and the realities of a world beyond, and we meet it when our curiosity has gone as far as normal answers can be given. Mystification, on the other hand, is the immediate offering of irrational material or ceremony as a substitute for thought and an escape from responsibilities. It would be easy to invent a new religion of mystification every day of the week—and sometimes it looks as though this is indeed happening in our day.

There's a story in the Old Testament about an odd thing that happened as the Israelites were in the desert after their Exodus from Egypt. They were complaining about the miserable conditions and suggesting to Moses that they had been better off as slaves. Whereupon he is said to have been promised by the Lord: "I will rain bread from heaven for you." And, sure enough, the next day, in the words of the Bible, "Behold, upon the face of the wilderness there lay a small round thing, as small as the hoar frost on the ground. And when the children of Israel saw it, they said to one another, It is manna: for they wist not what it was." A good name for an unknown substance—manna: what-is-it?

Now, of course, we could have told them. I find in the encyclopedia exactly what it is. "A study of the tamarisk production of manna in the valleys of central Sinai led to the conclusion that manna is produced by excretions of two closely related species of scale insects. A closer analysis of these excretions revealed that they contained a mixture of three basic sugars with pectin." So now we know, and the mystery disappears. Or does it? This manna for the Israelites was a sacrament of God's presence and protection. Its coming was a sign from the mystery beyond. For the people of God this sticky product of the desert became the symbol of the divine mystery and has entered into the imaginative life of the people of God, Jewish and Christian, ever since.

There's a passage in John where we hear Jesus referring to this manna and going on to speak about himself in strange and haunting words:

"Our fathers ate the manna in the wilderness; as it is written, 'He gave them bread from heaven to eat.'"

131

Jesus then said to them, "Truly, truly, I say to you, it was not Moses who gave you the bread from heaven; my Father gives you the true bread from heaven. For the bread of God is that which comes down from heaven, and gives life to the world." They said to him, "Lord, give us this bread always."

Jesus said to them, "I am the bread of life; he who comes to me shall not hunger, and he who believes in me shall never thirst." (John 6:31-35 RSV.)

Manna—what is it? Manna—who is it? If there was mystery in the feeding of the Israelites in the wilderness, there is even greater mystery in the coming of Jesus Christ into our world. It has to do with the greatest hunger that we ever know, the hunger for meaning, for hope, for a purpose in life, for a glimpse of the eternal as we stumble on. You cannot reduce such a revelation to a religious platitude. You cannot analyze the statement: "I am the bread of life" as if it were a scientific formula. Yet the curious thing is that millions have found in these words the deepest satisfaction life can afford. They need no other explanation than the discovery that Christ indeed can sustain us in our pilgrimage and nourish us with the inward presence of God himself.

If, then, he came to do this—to give us nothing less than the re-creating power that flows from the divine and the experience of an eternal life that begins now—then, of course, there was mystery about his birth. And how else can such mystery be expressed than through the poetry and the stories that cluster around the event of Bethlehem? The intellectually curious are welcome to investigate the records, deciding what is historical and what is legendary. But the spiritually curious will find themselves drawn into a world where shepherds hear angel music and tyrants tremble on their thrones. They will know that here something unique, something truly extraordinary, is happening; and they will know how to open not only the mind but the imagination to the divine visitation.

This is why as Christmas dawns each year I say let's keep the mystery. In the last chapter I quoted Ring Lardner: "Shut up! he explained." We might keep that in mind when the eye falls on the star of Bethlehem, or the ear takes in the familiar sound: "Come and behold him, born the king of angels." This is the moment for the intrusive voices of explanation to shut up so that we may hear the word of the Lord. And it may be that, in the traffic of a city street, or in the loneliness of an empty home, or in the automobile that is speeding you to your next engagement, or in a hospital bed, you may suddenly be still and know that this is God—God coming to you in the old familiar story of the birth of Jesus.

13

The Inquisitive Angel: A Christmas Reflection

From the beginning of this book we have examined various aspects of what I call "religious curiosity." My theme in this chapter is the same, but the treatment is, shall we say, a little offbeat. What I am giving you is a fantasy designed for children of all ages. By that I mean that it is cast in a form that may appeal to the child in every one of us, as well as to children. The full title of the story is "Archie, the Inquisitive Angel." And now we are ready to begin.

If everyone is very quiet, I'll tell you a story about an angel. It's only when we are quiet that angels come near. They don't like noises like taxi horns, jet planes, sneezes, cross voices, or crinkling candy papers. The only people who have ever heard the angels have been very still, like Mary, the mother of Jesus, alone in her room, or the shepherds in the frosty fields under the silent stars. If you ask me what angels look like, I have to say that I don't know—except that they don't have bodies like you and me. You can picture them any way you like, but I'll tell you a secret: they don't need wings. They can go anywhere they like without them. If there should be a grown-up who doesn't believe in angels, I'll just ask one question, and then we'll get on with the story. The question is: "Do you think that in the whole huge universe we human beings are the only living spirits who think, and pray, and love?" If you say, "Probably not," then you've opened the door for angels, and one of them might come in.

The one I'm going to tell you about is called Archie. If you ask me how I know he is called Archie, the answer is that I know because I gave him the name. And why shouldn't I give him the name? Lots of people have been giving angels names for thousands of years. You see there are only two angels with names in the Bible—Gabriel and Michael—so they have been inventing names for the others ever since. A friend of mine once published a book called a *Dictionary of Angels* —and do you know how many names of angels he has found? Three thousand, four hundred and six. So here comes Archie, and now there are three thousand, four hundred and seven.

His story begins so long ago that if you said, "A

billion years, a billion years, a billion years," without stopping from now till you went to bed you would not have counted back to the time I mean. In fact, you would have to run out of time altogether, for Archie's first adventure happened when there was no New York, no America, no world, no sun, no moon, no stars—just God and lots and lots of nothing at all, except for the angels. You might think that this would be very dull, and, I have to confess, Archie was a little bored. You see, all that went on was singing and praying, like a church service—and, though I hope you enjoy church services, I'm sure you wouldn't want to be singing hymns and praying twenty-four hours a day forever and ever. So when the great choirs were singing "Holy, Holy, Holy," Archie used to wink at a little cherub and say: "Roly-poly-poly; there must be something else to do." It wasn't that he wanted to run away from God. He knew what happened to dropouts: they became little devils. No, he wasn't a bad angel. He was just curious. He was sure that something else was going on, something exciting.

One day he was with a billion angels at a huge prayer meeting. Suddenly he heard away in the distance a big bang. "I wonder what that is," he said to himself; then slipped away as fast as he could. "Hi!" shouted the archangel, "where are you off to?" "Don't stop me now," said Archie. "Fly now; pray later." And off he sped through light-years and space-time and curved nothingness till he reached the point where the big bang had happened. By this time there were lots of other angels around, and to his surprise they were shouting for joy, just like a crowd in a stadium when the home team hits the winning run. "What's going on here?" asked Archie, for since he was very inquisitive that was his favorite question.

One of the angels stopped shouting long enough to say one word: "Creation." "Creation?" said Archie. "What's that?" "Look!" said the angel, and Archie saw that all around him things were happening—and that was exciting, for up to this moment there had been no things to happen. But now there were lots of things—vapors and gases and electrons and flashing lights and more big bangs. Archie got so excited he began to shout too, and it seemed that everything was caught up in a song he had never heard before. For God was creating the universe and all the heavenly family was dancing for joy. Archie was entranced. "Isn't it wonderful," he said over and over as he watched. A few billion years went past but Archie never noticed them, for angels, you know, are forever and ever. The vapors became solid. Huge masses went crashing off in all directions, and little chips flew off them and formed into rhythmic patterns—great galaxies of stars. "Wonderful, wonderful," said Archie, "something has happened at last. I wonder what becomes of all these little pieces that are floating around."

So off he went following a sun that was burning its way through space, and then as more little pieces began to break off he followed one of them and saw that it was spinning around its sun and something began to happen on it. "What's going on here?" said Archie, for he didn't know that he was watching our earth begin to come to life. Archie came nearer and nearer. The millions of years were spinning by, and he saw water and land and mud and trees and flowers. Then he saw something moving. "What's going on here?" said Archie, and came closer. There, on the earth, were hundreds of swimming things and creeping things and flying things and running things—fish and snakes and birds and animals. There were elephants and rhinoceroses and parrots and seals and eagles and saber-toothed tigers, so many strange shapes and colors and sizes that Archie drew a deep breath and said: "Isn't it wonderful!"

Only one thing puzzled Archie. He wondered why none of these animals could think the thoughts that he thought, why none of them could roam through the universe in his imagination, why none of them could really get to know the wonderful God who had made them all. Then one day he found animals that could do all these things. They were called Man and Woman. They could talk; they could think big thoughts; they could wander in imagination far beyond the earth; and they could talk to the great God and listen to what he

had to say to them. "Isn't that wonderful," said
Archie, and he went to an archangel and got permission to hover around the human family and see
what happened.

It was an exciting time for Archie. He watched
men build houses and make fire and hunt for food.
He saw them paint pictures, and he heard them
laughing as they danced and sang together. He saw
little children playing. He saw lots of love and
happiness and kindness. And he watched as men
and women and children tried to talk to God and
to give him presents. Then he began to notice something else. One day he heard an ugly noise. Never
before had he heard angry words and terrible
shouts, so he said to himself: "What's going on
here?" and hurried off to see. And what he saw
was enough to make an angel weep. For a crowd
of men were struggling together in a field, shouting vicious words at each other and hurling stones
and sharp sticks, so that many were lying dead and
wounded on the ground. They didn't want to
listen to God anymore. Each one wanted to be
the big boss and get more land, more food, more
things than anyone else.

Archie tried to figure it out. "I suppose something like this might have happened to me if I'd
gone away from God with the dropout angels," he
thought. "Now I wonder what God will do." So he
hung around, and he marveled that God was so
wonderfully patient with these men and women.

He kept showing them the way to live, kept talking to them, and every now and then one of them had an unexpected vision of God himself.

For instance, there was that day when Archie, as he hovered around the earth (angels are very good at hovering, you know), suddenly saw a company of angels with a long ladder. The top of it soared away up into the sky, while the bottom of it rested on a sleeping man. As a matter of fact it rested on his dream—for this was a dream ladder. "What's going on here?" asked Archie. "Ssh!" said the angels. "That's Jacob. He's having a dream and watching us going up and down from earth to heaven, and heaven to earth." So Archie started going up and down as fast as he could. "Isn't it wonderful," he said. "Look—he's waking up." And sure enough Jacob woke up and saw nothing but the wide desert and the stone he had used for a pillow. But he knew something had happened. "God was here," he said, "and God is going to do something wonderful for the human family."

So Archie went away and began to puzzle out what God could do that would be so wonderful. He could blot out all these foolish human beings and begin with another set altogether. Or he might show himself in such a terrifying way that they would all know who is really the Big Boss. Anyway, Archie was sure that they couldn't be allowed to go on doing evil and hurtful things for ever and ever.

A little later by Archie's time, but about two

thousand years by ours, he found the answer. Nobody on earth, and nobody in heaven, could ever have guessed what it would be. It was the most wonderful thing that happened since the exciting time of the Creation. Yet this time there was no Big Boss. This time there were no flashing lights, no zooming galaxies, no throbbing in the depths of space-time. But there was a chorus. And this is where Archie came in. On a quiet evening when the stars were bright he was hovering around a little corner of the earth when he discovered an angel choir singing the most lovely song he had ever heard. "What's going on here?" he asked. "Ssh!" said one, "don't you know this is the silent night, the holiest night this earth has ever seen? For God has come to bring to these poor mortals the peace and goodwill that they need." "How has he come?" asked Archie. "I don't see any heavenly armies. I don't hear any thunder of his voice. The world looks just the same to me as it ever was."

"Come," said the angel, "and you will see the love of God, the presence of God, the peace of God, right there among men." "But," said Archie, as they hovered nearer, "I don't see any palace. I don't see any throne. I don't see any temple. I see only a stable where oxen are feeding." "Look again," said the angel; and Archie saw a man and a woman crouching in the straw. "Look again," said the angel; and Archie saw, lying in the woman's lap, a tiny little baby, looking out on the world

141

with the bright and wondering stare of the newly born. "There," said the angel, "this is how God has come." There was silence in the stable except when an ox shifted in the stall, or the baby uttered a little cry. But the air was filled with angel voices; "Glory to God in the highest; and on earth peace, goodwill toward men." And Archie knew that his question was answered. God had done what no one could have ever imagined. He had given his Son to men, so that they might know his love and find his peace. "Isn't it wonderful," said Archie, "the most wonderful thing that has ever happened since it all began." The inquisitive angel was satisfied at last.

But not for long. In case you think that is the end of the story I have to tell you that Archie soon began to ask questions again. "I wonder," he said as the years went speeding by, "I wonder how men treated the Son of God; I wonder if they love him and follow him." So he went to ask Gabriel what happened. "Alas," said Gabriel, "they didn't treat him very well. When he grew up they listened to him for a while, but then they turned against him, ill-treated him, and in the end they killed him." "Killed him?" said Archie, horrified. "Yes," said Gabriel, "but there were some who loved him, and they found that he was alive again. And he is alive now, and still at work in the world." "Then," said Archie, "I must go and see what is happening." And by that time the years had gone slipping past, and it was—what do you think?—today.

So Archie came hovering down to our world. He went to Asia, to Africa, to the land where Jesus lived, to Europe, and to America. He went into people's homes. He walked the city streets. He read the newspapers. He watched television. "What's going on here?" he kept asking. And the answer was that in many places he heard angry words, he saw ugly sights, quarrels, and fighting, and it made him very sad. But there was something too that made him very happy. In every land he found men and women, boys and girls, who knew Jesus and who were following him. He saw them helping each other, healing the sick, feeding the hungry, trying to bring peace in families, in nations, and between nations. He heard a great chorus of praise and prayer rising to God in all kinds of languages in every land. "Isn't that wonderful," he thought to himself. "In spite of all the ugly things there is still a huge family of God's children who want to give him glory and to spread peace and goodwill among men."

Of course, Archie, like you and me, would like to know just when and how it is all going to end. But when, inquisitive as ever, he asked the question, the answer he got was: "Nobody knows; no, not even the angels in heaven." So Archie has to be content to hover around and help all those of us who want this world to be really God's family.

So you see the story really has no ending. For this Christmas and next year and in the years to come, from time to time all of us are going to hear a little voice asking: "What's going on here?" Am I on the side of love and peace and goodwill, or am I adding to the hatreds, the quarrels, the bitterness? And if sometime when you are feeling low and depressed about everything, suddenly a little flash of hope springs up and you find yourself saying: "Isn't it wonderful? Jesus is alive, and love will always win," then don't be surprised. It might be Archie.